Church Boy

by Kirk Franklin

WITH JIM NELSON BLACK

WORD PUBLISHING

NASHVILLE

A Thomas Nelson Company

This book is dedicated to my sister
Suwanna Smith.
Come home soon.

CHURCH BOY

Copyright © 1998 by Kirk Franklin. All rights reserved. No portion of this
book may be reproduced, stored in a retrieval system, or transmitted in any
form or by any means—electronic, mechanical, photocopy, recording, or
any other—except for brief quotations in printed reviews, without the prior
permission of the publisher.

Scripture quotations used in this book are from the New King James
Version (NKJV), copyright © 1979, 1980, 1982, 1992,
Thomas Nelson, Inc., Publisher.

Library of Congress Cataloging-in-Publication Data
Franklin, Kirk.
Church boy / by Kirk Franklin with Jim Nelson Black.
p. cm.
ISBN 0-8499-4050-8
1. Franklin, Kirk. 2. Gospel musicians—United States—Biography.
I. Black, Jim Nelson. II. Title.
ML420.F838A3 1998
782.25'4'092—dc21   98-20991
[b]   CIP
                                                                                MN

Printed in the United States of America
8 9 0 1 2 3 4 5 9 **QPV** 9 8 7 6 5 4 3 2 1

Contents

Acknowledgments

When the publishers at Word first approached me about doing this book, I must be honest and say I felt very nervous about such an idea. First, because I try to work very hard at not taking credit for things that I believe were totally God ordained. Second, because words like success and achievement make me feel very uncomfortable. Success for me is not the music but living every word of the music. So, to every reader I pray that I do not come across as arrogant, boastful, or proud but as a testimony that God and only God can take nobodies and use them for His glory. Last but not least, there are times when I become very transparent in this book. I have made a lot of mistakes in my life. I've struggled with my flesh and have hurt people who didn't deserve to be hurt. But I must be honest with myself, as well as with the reader, so that deliverance will come. Thank you, thank you.

This book is just a piece of my story because there are still pages to fill, mistakes to make, and lessons to learn.

To every pastor, bishop, and preacher who has poured into my life, thank you.

To Gerald, Jessie, and Diana, thank you for not holding me against me.

To the Family, God's Property, and every other Gospel artist, I am here to serve you . . . It is an honor.

To Vicki and the GospoCentric family, most of the chapters in this book are because of you. Thank you.

To my children, Kerrion, Carrington, and Kennedy, Daddy prays that he never lets you down. You've turned me from a boy and made me a man.

And to Tammy, Heaven had mercy on me and gave me you; I love you.

— KIRK FRANKLIN

P.S. To the reader, don't judge me until you've finished the book. Thank you.

Beginnings

(Part 1)

Don't give me a mansion on top of a hill,
Don't give me the world with a shallow thrill,
But just give me a Savior, my life He can mold,
I'd rather have Jesus than silver and gold.

I woke up this morning feeling kind of down,
I called on my best friend, he could not be found,
But I can call Jesus, my life He can mold,
I'd rather have Jesus than silver and gold.

Silver and gold, silver and gold,
I'd rather have Jesus than silver and gold.
No fame or fortune, no riches untold,
I'd rather have Jesus than silver and gold.

Silver & Gold

It was the first of November 1996, and there was a chill in the air. I had flown in from Kansas City that day for our concert in Memphis. By the time I drove from the airport to the auditorium downtown where the crew was setting up, most of the singers were already there. They had come in on the charter the night before. The musicians were onstage warming up, and there was a lot of activity and anticipation.

As usual, a catered meal was being served backstage before the show, so several people were standing around talking, joking, and eating when I arrived. I went around and spoke to everybody. I said hello to Fred Hammond and several of the band members and traded jokes with some of the younger performers traveling with us, then I grabbed a plate and sat down to eat with the Family.

There are a lot of gospel music fans in the Memphis area, and our promoter, Al Wash, who had flown in from Dallas that afternoon, told us the hall was already sold out. People were coming in for the concert by car and by bus from Arkansas, Mississippi, southwestern Tennessee, and all over the region. So we were happy and enthusiastic, and I was fired up and ready to go.

Sometime during the meal I said, "Something's going

to happen to us tonight—something that's going to change our lives forever." I don't actually remember saying those words, but several members of the Family told me later that I did. I believe now that, at that moment, the Lord must have been already showing me that something unusual and important was about to happen. He has shown me things like that before, and I trust His silent witness. But I didn't have any idea what that "something" was going to be that night.

Memphis was the third stop on our third road trip, the Tour of Life, and Yolanda Adams was the first artist in the lineup, to be followed by Fred Hammond and Radical for Christ. The usual routine was that I would come out with Fred and Yolanda at the beginning to get things rolling. As soon as Yolanda started her first number, I would leave and go back to my dressing room. Later I would come back on stage with all fifteen members of the Family, and we would do our show. Then, at the very end of the concert, everybody would join us for the big finale.

Things were hopping that night as I introduced Yolanda, handed off my microphone, and headed to the back. David Mann, a singer with the Family and one of my oldest friends, was standing nearby, and as I was leaving the stage I caught his eye and motioned for him to come with me. We needed to check on a few things, so David and I headed offstage together.

It was dark back there, and just as I was about to walk through the curtain, David looked back over his shoulder toward the audience. By the time he turned around again, I was gone. He couldn't figure out where I went, so he walked over to the curtain, pulled it back, and suddenly realized there was nothing there, nothing but a big, black hole—the pit behind the stage. When he saw it, David told me later, his heart literally stopped.

He couldn't see anything in the pit, so David yelled for some of the guys to come over. None of them could see anything either. Finally, Jessie Hurst, our road manager who has been with me from the very first, noticed the worried look on their faces, hurried over, looked into the pit, and said, "Man, forget this!" *And he just jumped down into the pitch-black darkness!*

Nobody could see anything in the black hole until someone finally turned on the backstage lights. Then they saw me, lying in a heap on the floor of the pit. And they realized that Jessie had landed just a couple of feet from my head. Now, Jessie is a pretty big boy, and if he had hit me, it probably would have been all over right there. He could have killed me just by landing on me, but later Jessie said he couldn't afford to wait any longer. If I had fallen into that pit he knew I had to be hurt, and he wasn't about to wait around, wringing his hands, waiting to find out.

I was covered with blood, not exactly conscious but not exactly unconscious either. They said I kept repeating, "Speak, Lord! Give me a word! Speak to me, Lord!" I kept saying it over and over until the ambulance and paramedics arrived, hooked me up with intravenous fluids, loaded me onto a stretcher, and took off for the hospital.

The emergency room doctors at Regional Medical Center transferred me almost immediately to the intensive care unit, where I was on life support for a while. For the next three and a half hours, I'm told, I was in and out of consciousness. I didn't appear to have any broken bones, the doctors said, but there was bleeding inside my skull, and they were concerned that I might have additional, even more serious, internal injuries.

Doctors said they didn't think my condition was going to be fatal, but whenever there is a serious head injury, they always use life support in case the patient should stop breathing. So I had tubes and wires and hoses stuck all over my body.

I have no memories of any of that, and maybe that's good! There are some things I don't want to know. I'm just glad those doctors made all the right decisions that night. And I'm glad to know God was with me through it all.

I have no doubt that Jesus took my hand and walked me through the fire. The devil wanted to stop me, to break me, to kill me. But he was way out of his league: I was in God's hands from the start. And if there was ever any doubt about that, then all doubts were erased that night as God's people began to pray for me.

A WORD FROM ABOVE

When I fell, nobody onstage or in the audience knew for several minutes that anything unusual had happened. Except for David, Jessie, and several members of the backstage crew who had helped direct traffic and guide the paramedics to where I had fallen, no one knew I was hurt, and those who did know didn't have any idea how bad my injuries might be.

During all this time, Yolanda was still onstage singing, and thousands of people were rejoicing and enjoying her music. Suddenly Fred Hammond, who had come back several times to see what was happening to me, realized that the greatest Helper of all wasn't far away. He hurried back on stage and motioned to Yolanda that he needed to have a word with the people. Yolanda stopped singing, raised her hand for silence, and motioned for the band to stop playing. When Fred took the microphone and explained that I had just fallen off the stage and was on my way to the hospital, a sudden rush of surprise and alarm went through the crowd. Fred asked for quiet then said that he felt the Spirit of the Lord calling all the people in the auditorium to start praying for me; he asked that they pray for God's hand of healing and protection on my life.

Then, for the next several minutes, Fred led the audience in the most anointed prayer you can imagine. When Yolanda told me about it later, she said, "Kirk, God just touched our hearts at that moment, and as Fred started praying, the feeling was so strong, so overpowering, that all over the music hall people were praying and crying out to God to spare your life."

A spirit of anointing seemed to come over the place, she said, and people began talking to the Lord, calling on the name of Jesus to pour out a blessing on me. The auditorium was filled with prayers and tears and anxious cries. I didn't know anything about any of that at the time, of course. But when they told me about it later, I thanked God that all those people had reached out in that way and prayed so fervently when I needed it the most. I have no doubt that God heard those prayers and used them to give me the strength to survive. What a wonderful act of mercy, and what an incredible testament to the power of faith.

Jon Drummond, my best friend and an outstanding athlete, was on the road with us during that particular trip. As soon as we got to the hospital, Jon realized that somebody was going to have to call my wife, Tammy, and let her know what had happened.

So Jon got to a phone and called her. He didn't want to scare her, however, because she was about fifteen weeks pregnant with our daughter Kennedy, so he really downplayed everything. He told Tammy that I had tripped onstage and hurt myself. He said they had taken me to the hospital just to check everything out.

Tammy was supposed to fly down to meet me in New Orleans the next day, but as gently as he could, Jon suggested, "Tammy, instead of waiting until tomorrow when we get to New Orleans, why don't you come on now. See if you can change your ticket and just come on to Memphis. I'm sure Kirk would like to see you now."

Over the next hour or so, Tammy and my manager, Gerald Wright, called the airline but could not get out until 6:00 the next morning. They flew in and came straight to the hospital to see how I was doing. Later, Tammy told me she wondered why people were trying to keep her away from any televisions or radios as they made their way to Memphis. She thought that was weird. But she *really* started to think something was strange when they got to the hospital and police officers and security guards were all over the place.

She noticed that, as soon as she came up to the hospital door, one of the officers held a walkie-talkie to his mouth and said, "We have Mrs. Franklin. She's here. We have her now." People were standing around, but Tammy said that when the officers took her inside, the crowd just parted, like the Red Sea. The hospital had also provided her with a nurse, and a chaplain was there, which frightened her. A chaplain was standard hospital procedure for trauma patients' families.

She thought that was really odd, and she wondered why people were staring at her as she and Gerald were going down the hall. But even with all that, she still didn't put two and two together. It wasn't until she saw the intensive care doors that she realized I was in ICU.

Then it hit her: My injuries were actually more serious than they had told her at first.

When it looked as if I wasn't getting any better, the doctors said they were going to drill a hole in my head to relieve the pressure that was building up as a result of the internal bleeding. They briefed Tammy on the procedure, and she authorized them to go ahead. But just as they were about to begin, I woke up! Everybody said it was a miracle, and it was clear that the hand of God had touched me.

I wasn't fully recovered, of course, not by any stretch of the imagination, but the doctors told Tammy they wouldn't have to go ahead with the procedure after all. I'm glad things took a positive turn at that moment—not only because of the risk of infections or other complications from that kind of surgery but also because it might have kept me off the stage for months, or even years.

The hospital was packed with friends and well-wishers for the first couple of days. My pastor, Bishop David Martin, flew in from Dallas and helped direct the flow of people around the waiting areas at the medical center. Jesse Jackson came to the hospital along with a local congressman from Tennessee, and former heavyweight champ Mike Tyson sent red roses to my hospital room.

Rhythm and blues star R. Kelly drove all the way from Chicago to see me. Shortly after Tammy and Gerald Wright arrived, the president of GospoCentric Records company, Vicki Lataillade, flew in from California with a couple of others.

Of course, I didn't know anything about those special visitors. I'm honored that so many people came to wish me well, but I was out cold most of the time, and whenever my eyes were open I wasn't really alert or coherent.

When the doctors finally got me stabilized, they made an assessment of my condition and called Tammy and her parents into one of the consulting rooms at the hospital. Gerald Wright and Vicki Lataillade were there too, along with one or two others, and they all sat quietly while the doctor gave them the prognosis.

He said I had fallen on the left side of my head, which is the side of the brain that controls all the creative functions. So there was a chance, he said, that I'd never be able to write music or perform again. There was also some concern that I'd never be able to think, write, or speak clearly, and he said I might have to go into physical therapy to learn how to talk all over again.

As you can imagine, everybody in the room was stunned by the doctor's words. They didn't know what to expect, but it sounded horrible. Then, finally, at one point the doctor said, "We managed to get a few words out of him today, but he stutters now."

Suddenly everyone who knew me started laughing. "He stuttered before!" they said.

"Oh, I see," the doctor said, a bit of relief showing on his face. I'm sure he must have been surprised by their reactions. But then he went on with the diagnosis. "Well," he said, "I also noticed that Mr. Franklin's voice is a little raspy."

This time my friends and family really started laughing: "Always was!" they said. "His voice has been raspy as long as we can remember!"

THE ROAD TO RECOVERY

That conversation helped lighten things up a little, and everyone started to feel a little better, just knowing that I was awake and speaking once again. They were trusting that God was in control. They knew He wouldn't let things get out of hand. They were right, of course. My recovery was nothing short of a miracle.

I found out eventually that thousands of people had been praying for me all through those difficult days, and I'll always be grateful for that. During the next several weeks, more than twenty thousand cards and letters of support came pouring in. It felt like the hand of God reaching down to me through all those beautiful people who wrote to encourage us. How can I ever thank all God's people who reached out to me with so much love and concern? I can't tell you what a blessing it has been for the Family and me to feel that kind of support from our friends, fans, and supporters.

Everybody was very kind and patient—especially my wife. Tammy was so helpful while I was recuperating, both in Memphis and after we returned home to Texas. It meant so much to me to see her devotion, even when she must have been going through a very emotional time. She took care of me and did whatever needed to be done, and that just made me love her more than ever. It was only later, when I was home resting, that she started teasing me, telling me I acted like a big baby!

The nurses would come in and say, "Can I get you anything to drink, Mr. Franklin?"

Tammy says I would just look up and say, "Ap-ple juice." She laughs whenever she says it! Here I was, a grown man, lying there like a big baby saying, "Ap-ple juice"! She even told me that I wasn't supposed to drive for a while but in that first week I sneaked out at three in the morning to get some Fruit Loops.

Well, if I was a big baby, I don't remember it! I don't remember anything about those first five days.

The one thing I do remember is that one day I just came out of it. It was like waking up from a long dream. One minute I was out there floating around in la-la land—who knows where I was?—and the next minute I was back.

I started talking to people and doing stuff as if everything were normal. I didn't realize what had happened, and I guess it would have been comic if my condition hadn't been so serious. I fell on a Friday night, and by the following Wednesday I was back among the living. After just five days, I was on my way to recovery. It was nothing short of a miracle.

I was improving daily, but I still was having monster headaches, and the doctors had to keep me sedated for several weeks. In addition to blood loss and other injuries, I also suffered a brain contusion, which, I'm told, is a serious bruise that involves damaged tissue, swelling, and internal bleeding. So the doctors said I needed lots of rest, and I had to take medications to reduce the internal pressure and relieve the pain.

I can say one thing for certain—I've never had headaches like that before or since. If it weren't for the medication, I don't think I could have survived the pain—apple juice or not!

If you believe the headlines—and I usually don't—the

world of gospel music went into shock for a couple of days after my fall. Somebody told me I was featured on the evening news on radio and television stations all over the country that night.

Since then, some people have suggested that the accident in Memphis actually launched my career. We were a good group before that, they say, but it was the fall that got people talking about Kirk Franklin and the Family in living rooms all across America.

Maybe that's true. I can't say. But if so, maybe that's what God was doing all along, and maybe that's why I felt that something big was about to happen to us that night. I don't know about that. But I'm convinced the fall wasn't just an accident. And it wasn't just *my* accident. I believe the fall was for all of us—for me, Tammy, the Family, all of us. We've learned a lot through that experience.

It isn't that anything about me or about my music has changed because of Memphis. The fall didn't make me a more godly man, as some people have said. I wasn't having trouble at home before that. Tammy and I were close and very happy together before and after the fall. And it wasn't as if I needed some kind of accident or tragic event to renew my love for God. I have always considered my music a ministry, so that didn't change after the fall.

The fall did make me stronger in some ways, however. I think it gave me a renewed sensitivity and a new intensity for what I do. But I would not say that it made me what I am today. I've seen some of the headlines and the magazine articles written by well-meaning reporters saying that the fall in Memphis turned my career around. But people who say that don't really understand what was happening at that time.

Before the accident, I always included a bit of dialogue in the program in which I would say, "God is bigger than any accident or illness or injury you may have. He can heal your heart, your soul, your body, and your mind. There's nothing God can't do if you'll let Him." The fall didn't change that speech. I still say it, and I still mean it. But today it has new meaning for me. Today I have the living proof that those words are true.

Even if God hadn't healed me, that wouldn't mean that He couldn't heal. The experience I've been through since that night in November 1996 is teaching me that if I have something now it's because God wants me to have it. If I'm enjoying some measure of success in the music world, it's because that's what God has in mind at this moment. It's not my plan. It's His plan, and it's what He is doing in and through the music and the message that counts.

I love what Paul said in Philippians: "For I have learned in whatever state I am, to be content: I know how to be abased, and I know how to abound. Everywhere and in all things I have learned both to be full and to be hungry, both to abound and to suffer need" (4:11–12). That's what I mean. That what it's all about. I have given my life to God, and He has the freedom to use my time and my talents any way He wants to.

You may remember that right after that passage in

Philippians, Paul wrote those words that are so important to anyone who's trying to live the Christian life in this world: "I can do all things through Christ who strengthens me" (v. 13). That's the strength that allows us to be conquerors.

It's not my strength; it's His. It's not my goal; it's His. And because it is, Jesus gives me the strength to be what I have be, the strength to do what I need to get done. That realization has been an important lesson for me.

FIRST THINGS FIRST

Most of the hype that has come out about my accident and what's happened since then is just that—hype. One of the main reasons I agreed to write a book about my life and music was to set the record straight and to let people know that the popular image of Kirk Franklin is not really who I am.

But this is not a book about Kirk Franklin and the Family or how great and important we think we are. No way! I'll leave all that to some of the reporters and media who like to indulge in sensationalism. This is not a book about my lucky breaks or how our sound caught on and launched some kind of gospel music sensation.

But this is supposed to be my story, and there are a few things I want you to know about me. I have not achieved—nor do I ever want to achieve—the mentality that I've arrived, that I'm successful, or that I'm better than where I've come from. I never want to come across as a young man who's gotten caught up in all the media hype.

That's one thing I never want to get into, and it's easy to do in this business if you're not careful. The world will celebrate with you and applaud you today then chew you up tomorrow, and I'm not interested in any of it. So let's just be real.

No, my story is not about success or fame or personal glory or anything like that. First of all, I don't buy any of that stuff. And second, that's not the real payback I'm seeking.

The payback that interests me is not the gold and platinum records on the wall or the money in the bank but the way Jesus can change a young man's heart, heal a young girl's hurts, and transform people's lives. Whenever a young person hears something in my music that opens his or her eyes to what it's all about, that's what turns me on. There's only one treasure that lasts, and that's the knowledge that I belong, body and soul, to Him.

So this is a book about people. And because of that, it's a book about hopes and dreams, about problems and hardships, and about how barriers can be broken down. It's about victory and how, through faith, all things work together for good.

I would also like this to be a book about the kinds of doubts and fears that so many young people are dealing with today—about the negative stuff being thrown in their faces and how the church needs to do a better job of responding to that. The world is always telling young people what they can't do, but God sees what they can do. We can do all things through Christ who strengthens us. That's what gets me excited!

So, first of all, the story of my life and music is the story of a young man who grew up in God's house, making music and sometimes traveling too fast. Sometimes I got ahead of myself and ahead of God's plan for me. I can't deny that, and I don't want to.

I have to admit that there were periods in my life when I was not living in the will of God, not walking the walk. And there were times when the life I was living was hurtful to me and to others. I regret all that now, more than I can say. But God brought me out of it and put my feet on higher ground, and that's what I want people to hear.

Most of all, I want this to be a book about how faith still moves mountains. It's about how God defeats all the negative stuff and gives people hope. This is a book about possibilities and how—with perseverance and determination—we really are conquerors.

If the story of Kirk Franklin were nothing more than some glorified press release about how I came to be written and talked about like some sort of musical sensation, it wouldn't be worth the paper it's printed on. And it certainly wouldn't be what's on my heart. There's so much more to it than that. I know, without a doubt, that God prepares the way for His messengers. And when I see how He has used the hurts and losses and pains of my past to shape the voice and the message of my music, I'm truly humbled.

God laid the tracks for this journey, then He used certain people and events to give me the exposure. That's part of my story. He put certain people—like that young record company president, Vicki Lataillade—right where they needed to be (and wanted to be) so the message could get out.

God sent people like Vicki to be part of my story. In every case, they were people who shared the same faith, the same convictions, and the same determination to break down barriers and touch people with God's love. They also believed that something big was about to happen.

I really mean it when I say that I love our traditions from years gone by. I have said that in concerts for years, and it's the truth. I love my people and the things they've taught me about faith, family, and freedom. I love our music and rich history—our African-American roots, our gospel songs, and especially the wonderful hymns of the churches I grew up in. I wouldn't be here today if it weren't for all those things.

But the world of the 1990s is not the world I grew up in. There are a lot more traps for young people now than there were when I was a kid. It was bad then, but the world, the flesh, and the devil have laid death traps for kids today, and the old ways, the old traditions, don't touch them anymore like they used to touch me when I was younger. That's why we're losing so many of them. If some of the churches and parents had done a better job, we wouldn't be seeing all the gang-banging going on out there.

You don't have to believe me. Check out the headlines! Check out the newspapers! Young black men—and young black women too—are under unbelievable pressures from society. They're being exploited by other people, by the media and the movies, and especially by the street culture. Whether it's the gangsta thing or this crazy consumer madness that's preying on everybody, they're into it, and it's eating them up. And it's not just within the black race; we're losing our kids, period.

Why? Because of the pressures of life and because of the bitterness that has grown up around them—and in them. I've seen it all across America, in every town where I've been on tour with the Family. Young people are making bad choices, and it's killing them. Drugs, crime, sexual promiscuity, AIDS—you name it. It's everywhere, and it's killing them.

My point is not to say that it's hopeless, because I'm convinced it isn't hopeless. But yesterday's way of dealing with these problems isn't working. The good news is that God hasn't given up! So we can't afford to give up either.

SOME HARD FACTS

I think it's important to deal with some of the issues facing young people, like the fact that some traditional churches have not been as sensitive in the past as they could have been to people like me. Some African-American churches—which is the only church I know very much about—have not dealt with the source of the problems facing our culture today.

It's the same in the white church, the brown church,

the Asian church. And if we're losing our young people in all these places, then isn't it about time that we all started turning some corners? We don't need riots or race wars or protest marches to do this job. We don't need a political party. What we need is a Holy Ghost party, and there's no better time than right now to get one started!

There are some people who wish I wouldn't say these things, but I have to say them. In every major city in this country, wherever we have traveled on tour, young people have come up to me after the show to tell me about their fears and concerns. They tell me they're hurting, and I care about that.

If I have to be a rebel, then that's what I'll do. But I'm a rebel with a cause. Even in gospel music I've been considered a rebel. But I'm a rebel who wants to see what can happen to America and to the church when we start doing things God's way for a change.

I don't believe in a particular musical sound, but I do believe in a particular message. Regardless of the beat or the groove, the music has to draw us to the cross. That's the real reason for the existence of gospel music in the first place. If it doesn't do that, then I'd say it's a failure, regardless of the sound.

If our music only gets people excited and doesn't plant a seed that will eventually lead to salvation, then I'm wasting my time. But if the message is not compromised, then people shouldn't give us a hard time about the type of sound we make.

I also think it's important to speak up about what some

of our pastors are saying but not doing out there. A big scandal in the papers a couple of months before this book went to press concerned the president of a black Baptist denomination in Florida who was apparently living a double life. When his people found out what was going on, they didn't give him a hard time. They just closed their eyes and said it was okay.

Is that how it's supposed to be? Is that what Jesus would say? I have to ask myself: If the church isn't real and if Christians aren't living the life, then who else is going to do it?

We all know people who have not been living what they've been preaching. Like a lot of people in the church today, I've been a victim of that. I've been around pastors who have not lived what they've preached. There was a time when I lived that kind of life myself, always trying to explain why I wasn't what I appeared to be. But that has changed now. With God's help, I've turned the corner, and I'm never going back. There's too much at stake, and Christ has opened my eyes to some hard facts.

I can honestly say that there was a time when I didn't see anything wrong with the way I was living because nobody else did either. Nobody said anything. Nobody pointed a finger, and nobody seemed to care. Now I'm here to say that there are a lot of hurt people out there because too many Christians have preached a good gospel without living the life, but that has got to change.

The church has got to be real. So I say, let's take off the

doctrines and the bylaws and the sanctimonious speech, and let's just get back to basics. We've got to be transparent before God so we can be the people of God. How else can we hope to get people ready for Christ's return?

We've got to be spiritually transparent and emotionally naked before God. One reason we're losing so many young people to Satan and the allure of this world is because they don't want to be what we've made ourselves appear to be. Even if they want to live by a higher standard, they don't like what they see in us. They don't think they can live by impossible rules, so they don't even try.

I want to reach nonbelievers in nontraditional ways. I want to see revival come back to this land. Those are all things we need to talk about, and we need to talk about the war being waged for the hearts and minds of young people today.

The Bible says it's up to us to work out our own salvation with fear and trembling. Paul wrote in Philippians, "It is God who works in you both to will and to do for His good pleasure" (2:13). God is calling each of us, and He has a plan for us. But we've got to keep ourselves humble. We've got to keep ourselves focused.

My message to young people is, don't be looking to somebody else to solve your problems. Teachers and preachers can't make you good. The police department can't make you good. Government can't clean up your act. Nobody else can get you back in touch with God but you.

You've got to deal with your own negative upbringing.

Government can't do it for you. *Nobody* can do it but you. Look to Jesus. He can take the wounds and the scars in your life and turn them into blessings. If you take the first step, God will bless it. No matter how small a step it is, He can handle it. He has given you the right to choose heaven or hell. So which will it be? Only you can make that decision.

Whenever God makes you choose, it's always out of His wrath. And there's no blessing if you're doing something from God's wrath. But if you're doing it from obedience, because you love Him and you want to please Him, that's when you receive the blessing.

Sooner or later, we've got to break down the walls between black and white people, and between gospel and contemporary Christian music. Racism keeps them there, but God's love can break them all down. The walls have to come down if we're children of the King. We've been *talking* about those walls coming down for years, but now they've *got* to come down.

Unfortunately, I believe racism will continue to exist until the black church and the white church get real, not only with each other, but with themselves. Racism in the church, and in the world, will remain until the children of God start dealing with their differences.

Of course, there is a difference between black people and white people, and anybody who says there isn't is being totally unrealistic. But that doesn't give either race license to turn up our noses or snarl at each other or even to just ignore one another. It's not enough to say we believe in unity and brotherhood if we turn around and do something else behind closed doors. We've got to become transparent—transparent in both our contemporary Christian music and black gospel music—admit that racism exists, and believe that something can be done about it. And we've got to open up in every area of our lives.

Yes, there's racism in both the black church and the white church. We are all guilty of resentment and divisions. But it won't change until Jesus comes—unless you and I begin to get real, right now, right where we are. Nobody can do that for us. We have to do it ourselves, and we need the grace of God to give us the strength and the will power to do what we know we have to do. Otherwise, others with a charismatic message will come and steal our glory.

THE MESSAGE IN THE MUSIC

I don't want this to be just a book about gold records or Stellar Awards or Grammys or any of the media recognition the Family and I have experienced the last few years. It's not about doing things the world's way. Instead, I hope the story of my life and music will demonstrate how God can take a kid from the inner city, give him a message, and used him to be a light—because it's the message in the music that really counts.

This is not a book about how great I am; it's a celebration of how great God is. It's about how God can take the imperfect gifts of imperfect people and turn them into silver and gold.

Riverside

It's Friday and my bills are due;
My three-month-old baby needs some shoes.
Can you feel what I'm going through?

Clock on the wall keeps tickin' tockin',
No stoppin' and somebody's knockin',
On the door, tellin' me to go.

My brother, I can't take no more,
So with my knees I hit the floor,
And say, "Help me, Jesus; help me, Jesus!"

Let's go down by the riverside.
Leave your problems all behind.
You can rest your troubled mind
Down by the riverside.

If I concentrate on all the bad
And all the things I wish I had,
How can the dark clouds ever pass?

Weeping may endure for a night,
But joy comes in the morning light;
God'll keep your spirit right.

So no matter what the people say,
Ain't nobody takin' this joy away.
In spite of everything I've been through,
I can say, "Thank You, Jesus; thank You, Jesus!"

2

They Need to Know

Some people say I was a blessed child, a musical prodigy, born to play the piano; therefore, all the things that have happened in my life and musical career were just the result of growing up the way I did. That's what they say, anyway. Others have said that I got a lot of lucky breaks along the way, as if everything that's happened for Kirk Franklin and the Family the past five years is just some sort of crazy accident or some quirk of fate.

Maybe that makes a good story, but unfortunately, neither version is entirely true or entirely fair. And if that's all you've heard about my life and music, then I think you're missing the real miracle of what's been going on the last few years.

The truth is, I've lived a hard life, right from the beginning, and right on the edge of poverty most of the time. If I hadn't fallen off that dark stage in 1996, there's a chance that most people still wouldn't know my name. But I'm convinced that God had a plan, not just in the fall, but in the music. As long as I can remember, He has been the number one thing in my life, and I know that nothing in my life has ever happened by accident.

Kirk Franklin

I was a child of the seventies, and believe me, I looked like it! Check out the picture of me at four years old in my white suit! Wide collars, big smile. If you've ever seen those old pictures of Sammy Davis Jr. tap-dancing for the cameras when he was about that age, or if you can remember the photos of Donny Osmond in his little white suits and wide, seventies-style collars, then you get the picture. That was me: big teeth, big smiles, playing the piano and singing like I knew what I was doing!

That part of my story has been told before, and everybody seems to like the "prodigy" part of it.

When my grandmother died, my birth mother was only about fifteen years old, and she was growing up to be pretty wild. Gertrude Franklin was my grandmother's sister and she felt an obligation to give her niece, Deborah, a place to stay; so she brought her over to live with her for a while. It was while she was living there, at Gertrude's house, that Deborah got pregnant with me.

Gertrude helped take care of me during the day and baby-sat me and looked after me at night whenever Deborah was out, which was most of the time. So Gertrude recognized the situation I was in from the start. She could see that Deborah didn't know what she was doing and that she wasn't going to be a very good mother.

One day she confronted her and said, "Deborah, if you're not going to take care of that baby, then give him to me. I'll adopt him and raise him right."

Church Boy

That's what happened. The adoption went through without a hitch, and a little while later Deborah moved out. Gertrude Franklin took on the job of raising a little boy, and she kept her word. She raised me right, and she loved me from the start. She made sure I always had whatever I really needed, and I bless her for that!

For a sixty-four-year-old woman who thought most of the hard stuff was behind her, that must have been a brave thing to do. But she did it without complaining. Her only child had been stillborn many years earlier; so I became Gertrude Franklin's baby, her only child, and she gave me all the love, attention, and discipline she knew how to give. She also gave me a sense of direction for most of my growing-up years. We went through some tough times, believe me, and we didn't always see eye-to-eye. She threw me out of the house more times than I can remember!

But Gertrude was dependable. She was as steady as a rock, and as I sang on our second album, "I loved her so—more than you'll ever know!"

Gertrude took me to church on Sundays, Wednesdays, and lots of other days, so I'd always know the bottom line. When she couldn't afford to buy me school clothes, she'd make them by hand. She sent me off to school on the bus each day so I would get an education. But Gertrude and her first husband, Jack Franklin, also exposed me to something else that changed my life.

Nobody could have guessed it would have the effect that it did, but Jack Franklin was a piano player. He played jazz and hymns and all kinds of popular music, and he even made a living at it sometimes. He was a deacon in the church, and I'm told he had an awesome voice. People who knew him say he was "good people."

Gertrude told me that when Jack played that old upright piano at our house, I was hypnotized. I'd sit at Jack's feet—or sit on his knee whenever he'd let me—and I'd just listen as long as he would keep playing. I was Jack's biggest fan! I'd clap my hands or dance or sing along with the music. When Jack would get tired and stop for the night, Gertrude said, I'd start screaming and kicking and pitching a fit!

But one day I crawled up on the bench and started picking around until I found out how to make sounds like the ones I'd heard Jack playing. At least, that's how I think it happened—I don't remember much about it! But by the age of four I was doing something that people called "playing the piano."

That was when Gertrude realized I was probably going to be a musician someday. At least, she said that's when she decided she needed to make arrangements for me to take piano lessons from a lady in our neighborhood.

Most of the time she could barely afford to pay the light bill, so to raise the extra money for piano lessons she had to go out and gather up aluminum cans along the roadside. On weekends and evenings, we'd walk up and down the street, looking in wastebaskets for used cans. Then we'd take them down to the recycling center and sell them for cash.

Church Boy

TOUCHED BY AN ANGEL

How do you thank somebody for that kind of care and concern? I'm not sure you can. Due in large part to Gertrude's love and courage, the first steps of my music career came a lot sooner than anybody expected. I was playing the piano by the age of four, and I've been performing in churches and with music groups of one kind or another ever since. I can't remember a time when I wasn't involved in music in some way.

Any maturity I have today can be credited to that sixty-four-year-old woman who adopted me when I was just three years old. That woman—what can I say? When I look back on it now, I begin to see the impact she had on my life, and there are times when I don't even believe she was from this earth.

Talk about "Touched by an Angel"! I *have* been! I believe Gertrude Franklin was put here on this earth for a few years to try to pour some stuff into my soul, to keep me out of prison, out of gangs, out of drugs. And I thank God for that.

She wasn't a super-mom. She wasn't perfect. Gertrude didn't have all the answers, and she didn't always come racing to the rescue when I got into a scrape. Sometimes her rescues were pretty blunt. She'd say, "You got yourself into this mess, young man. Now get yourself out!"

She could be tough, but what she did do was just what I needed at the time. And what she didn't do, I honestly believe, God never planned for her to do in the first place.

Gertrude focused me. She pointed me toward the good things, toward the church, and toward music. She did the best she could to steer me away from things that could have destroyed any future hopes I might have had. At one point I resisted that, and I got myself into a lot of trouble as a result. But Gertrude did her best, and she gets the credit for anything good I've ever done.

Despite all the love that Gertrude Franklin poured into her little boy, I wasn't a very secure child. As I was growing up, I became self-conscious and embarrassed about the way we lived. Not only were we poor and not only was my mother an old lady with a beat-up old car and a ramshackle old house, but I was shorter than most of the children my age. The big kids liked to beat me up all the time, just for fun.

I remember Gertrude being in church all the time. I remember her singing to me in the kitchen all the time. I also remember being the kid the other kids never liked. I was liked by some of the adults, all right, mainly because I was musical. But that wasn't always enough.

Some of the grownups thought I was cute—I must have seemed gifted to be playing the piano at such an early age. But to the other kids and to the parents of those kids, I wasn't gifted at all, and they didn't like me.

Even at church there were bullies who would drag me downstairs to the basement and beat me to a pulp while their parents were upstairs praising the Lord! That didn't do a lot for my self-esteem!

Church Boy

When I was ten years old, we had to move our membership to another church because the bigger kids started beating up on me so bad and so often. Now, you need to understand that changing churches was a real sacrifice for Gertrude, because she had been a member there since long before I was ever born. But she did it for my sake because she could see that what was happening wasn't good for me — or my soul.

She owned a hat shop on Evans Avenue in Fort Worth, where she made her living. In addition to making hats, she would take in sewing. She was a good seamstress, and she used to make my clothes. She made my little suits, and she also made the little knickers I had to wear.

Man, I hated those knickers! The boys would tease me, calling me a sissy and telling me I had legs like a girl because I had chubby little legs. But Gertrude made me wear those dumb knickers because she thought they made me look so cute!

Yes, I even had the white booties and the white socks that came up to my knees. That might have been fine for a baby, but Gertrude kept dressing me like that long after everybody else my age was wearing blue jeans and Jellies. Those little suits may have looked cute to her, but they got old for me real fast! And Gertrude's insistence on keeping me all dolled up had me in hot water with the other kids most of the time.

Gertrude used to go to the senior-citizen center when I was a boy, and she was involved in all kinds of activities there. She liked to crochet, and she loved to go bowling. For extra money, she would do housework for a wealthy white family who owned a car dealership in Fort Worth. It's not easy being a housekeeper for other folks, but they treated her well. They really liked Gertrude, and they treated me well too.

I always used to make her laugh with jokes and impersonations of famous people. She thought it was hilarious when I would do my Richard Nixon imitation. I'd put my hands up in the "V for victory" sign and shake my head like Nixon, and she would just throw back her head and laugh. I guess I was always basically a clown!

Even though I was formally adopted by Gertrude, I still had a distant relationship with my birth mother, Deborah, and I would see her from time to time. She would come by the house every month or two, but in reality she seemed more like a distant aunt than a mother to me.

People reminded me that Deborah was my birth mother, but the woman who took care of me, who loved me, and who sacrificed for me was Gertrude Franklin. That's what I was trying to say in "Mama's Song." I wanted to express the sense of relationship we had when I was growing up.

It wasn't meant to be a deep song, and it wasn't written for performance. I wrote it for Gertrude's funeral, and I think it touches on the special bond between us. I never planned to use that song in concert, but Vicki Lataillade talked me into using it on the *Whatcha Lookin' 4* album.

Church Boy

A SENSE OF CALLING

I always knew I was going to do something in ministry someday, and when I was four years old I told Gertrude I was going to be a preacher when I grew up. I don't remember very much about it or how it happened, but suddenly one day I felt I had a calling from God, and I knew He was going to use me someday to spread the gospel.

Gertrude reminded me later that I was sick that day, lying on the couch in the living room, watching a TV special about Dr. Martin Luther King Jr. That would have been around 1974, six years after Dr. King's assassination. After I watched the whole thing, I sat up and told Gertrude I was going to be a preacher. She didn't think much about it at the time, she said, but she didn't forget it either.

One thing that influenced me, I believe, happened when I was very small. I remember having stomach cramps a lot when I was a little boy, and sometimes I would get the twitches. I would start shaking from head to toe, and there was nothing we could do to make it stop. Basically they were just leg spasms, I guess, but whenever Gertrude would take me in to ask the doctor what was going on, he'd just say there was nothing he could do about it.

Having the twitches was very uncomfortable and frightening for me, and Gertrude and I were both worried that the spasms might be an indication of something more serious. But after another unproductive trip to the doctor's office, I said, "Mama, I know what we can do."

She said, "What's that, child?"

I said, "We can pray, Mama."

Well, Gertrude was a woman of faith, so she didn't hesitate. She went to the kitchen and got down her bottle of olive oil. She anointed me with oil and prayed over me. Sure enough, the twitches stopped, and they never came back after that. I knew then, and I think she knew too, that I had been healed of the condition, whatever it was.

Even then, in that situation as a very small child, I had faith that God was real and that He was a God of miracles. Since that time, I've always known that one day, one way or the other, I would be serving Him with my talents.

After I told Gertrude that I wanted to preach, I decided I needed to go down and talk to the pastor at our church about my decision. So one Sunday, during a special evening service, I went down to the platform and said, "Hey, I want to preach."

We were in a revival at the time, and I didn't think the preacher would do anything right away. But at the end of the sermon he told the congregation that there was somebody in the church that night who had come forward and said he was called to preach. I'm sure he must have played the whole scene for dramatic effect. Nobody knew who it was going to be, and I'm positive nobody suspected it was going to be a little boy!

Anyway, he pulled a chair up to the pulpit, pulled the microphone down a little bit, and then he came over and lifted me up and stood me on the chair. I gave the benediction that night. Gertrude said she nearly fainted when she saw me up there at the pulpit. She thought I was off playing with the other kids somewhere. She didn't even know I was in the building, let alone that I was going to give the closing prayer!

That was an unforgettable moment and, at least for Gertrude, a mixed blessing.

Things continued just fine for Gertrude and me until I was ten or eleven years old. That was when I started doing all the little-boy stuff that drives grownups crazy. It wasn't so much that I was an adolescent on my way to becoming a teenager or that I was some kind of horrible kid. I wasn't. I was just changing, and Gertrude didn't like it.

I was becoming a man. I stopped wearing the cute little suits. I think she was afraid that if I grew up I wouldn't be her little baby anymore. Now that I'm older and Gertrude is gone, I'm convinced that part of the reason for the tension between us during those years was that Gertrude couldn't deal with the fact that her baby was going to be a man someday.

I wish it could have been different. I wish I could have reassured her somehow. I wish she could have been a little more understanding or that I could have developed in some way that seemed less challenging and less upsetting to her. But the changes had to come. And whether she liked it or not, I couldn't be Gertrude's baby forever.

I understand why she worried. We lived in a rough neighborhood, and some of the stuff I was getting into was pretty risky. We both knew that. For example, there was a time when all the boys in my neighborhood would go down to the skating rink on Friday and Saturday nights. That's where all the action was.

Reluctantly, Gertrude let me go. Thanks to the money I was making as music director at Mount Rose Baptist Church, I had more than enough to get in and buy myself something to drink. But if I came home at 12:01 instead of 12:00 on the dot, that was a major problem. No matter how often it happened and no matter how loudly I protested, the results were always the same, and Gertrude always won!

She could see that I was pushing, stretching, trying to grow up, so Gertrude tried to get me involved in other things. She signed me up for Cub Scouts, Boy Scouts, Boy's Club, you name it. I was even involved in gymnastics for a while, but that didn't last long. The only thing that seemed to occupy my energies was music, so she tried to keep me active in music programs at our church.

Up until the age of eleven, I would sing and play the piano at church for all the programs, but one day just after my eleventh birthday the pastor asked me if I'd like to lead the choir. The church had recently lost their music minister, and the pastor thought it might be interesting—and maybe good for us—to see what a talented little boy could do. So he told the congregation I was going to be the new music leader, and they started to laugh.

Some of them yelled out, "Oh, come on! He's just a little boy!" But then I went up on stage, and before long we were doing some good music.

I was a kind of novelty act, I suppose. But don't get the

idea that everybody at Mount Rose Baptist Church was happy about it, because there were people in the choir who had grandchildren older than I was. For a little while I thought there was going to be some kind of revolt or a mass walkout. But they finally agreed to give it a try, and before long I think they realized it might actually work. The congregation responded to the idea, and the choir came around. They liked the music, and pretty soon they agreed to give me the job as the regular music director.

It was a gradual process, but now I realize what a powerful impact those experiences had on my life. I literally grew up performing in public. All the time I was singing and playing and leading music, I was also gaining experience and composure.

I was discovering how to hold people's attention, and I was pushing myself to do more and better stuff all the time. In fact, that's why I started writing music in the first place—to fill out a program or to develop some theme that we needed for a choir special. So all those experiences gave me a sense of responsibility, and they taught me how to be a music leader.

But, as I say, it wasn't all roses at Mount Rose either. There were some pretty hard times. There were times when I would try too much or times when I said things that the older people would interpret as being insensitive or rude.

You know I would never have said or done anything deliberately to hurt anybody, but some of the old folks were easily offended by the things I would say or do, and that was painful for all of us. Ultimately, I think they realized I was doing about as good as anybody else had ever done in the job. So they let me stay. And I stayed until I was eighteen years old and near the end of high school.

By that time I was into my rebellious teenage years.

GROWING UP TOO FAST

When you give your life to Christ, you're supposed to start growing into the image of Christ. You're supposed to know what's happening and start living so that God will be pleased with you. I wanted to live so that God could always point to me and say, "See, that's one of Mine! He's doing the things that please Me."

But, I'm sad to say, that wasn't always the way it was.

I think the enemy was trying to plant some seeds in me, even when I was just a little kid—some fleshly thorns. I was just a baby, two years old, when Gertrude's husband, Jack, was diagnosed with terminal cancer. He was in the hospital off and on for quite a while, but eventually they sent him home. Then the nurses would come over to the house and look after him during the day.

Gertrude told me that one day I wandered into the room, crawled over to where one of the nurses was standing and started rubbing her leg. She let out a shriek and Gertrude came running to see what was happening. She said she knew then that she was going to have to keep her eyes on that little boy!

Church Boy

"Oh, Lord," she'd say, "that baby is gonna break my heart someday if I don't watch him every minute!"

She watched me, all right, but as I grew older I really began to wrestle with temptations of the flesh. Like most kids, I was curious about what that stuff was all about, and I'm sorry to say I let my curiosity get the best of me more often than I'd like to admit.

Even as a little child I wrestled with the flesh. I have a half-sister, and we both struggled with the same sorts of things. I was lucky enough to be adopted by a woman who loved me and took good care of me. But my sister wasn't so lucky, and she told me after we were both grown that she struggled with the flesh even more than I did.

I think that another reason I got into so much trouble with sexual temptations during those years was that I was trying to fight my "image." I didn't talk about my church activities very much at school, but some of the kids found out about them and started teasing me. They called me "Church Boy."

I didn't mind so much when they called me "Church Boy." But they also called me "Mama's Boy" and started making jokes that I was gay, and that was painful. In the church, especially the African-American church during the seventies and eighties, homosexuality was a big problem. It still is in some places.

It's a problem today in gospel music—a major concern—and everybody knows it. Part of the trouble many artists have in gaining the acceptance of the church is that a lot of people just assume we're promiscuous and probably homosexual. We're not, but it's out there.

Homosexuality seems to be very common in the arts crowd, and I don't know why that should be. It seems that more than half the young people involved in dance, music, and the theater are openly gay. In fact, wherever people are talented and expressive there seems to be a tendency toward homosexuality, and the gospel music scene has not been exempt from that.

I wasn't gay, but running from the image got me even more involved with girls.

I used to go down to Gertrude's hat shop to hang out in the afternoons. But just down the street from her store there were some project-type apartments, and some of those girls would come up to see me. There was always the kind of activity going on that a boy my age shouldn't have been exposed to, but I was curious and went along with it sometimes.

The problem was that everybody I knew was messing around, and anytime I'd wonder if the stuff I was doing was bad, the other kids would say, "Yo, son, that's what's up!" Not only did they not condemn what I was doing, but they actually applauded it. And most of them were probably doing the same thing—or worse. Still, it's not something I'm proud of.

I don't mind being honest about this, because I believe that deliverance comes from being transparent and that a lot of times deliverance means resting in your testimony. I want people to know they can have victory over temptation. I admit I've made mistakes in the past, but God has given me a new start and a clean slate.

Today I encourage young people to make a promise before God and their peers to stay away from sexual sin. It can be very tempting, and it can look exciting, but you'll be sorry if you give in to it. Young people need to know that the enemy is a liar who wants to break their hearts and destroy their lives.

Don't let him have the satisfaction of defeating you!

THE MAIN THING

You know, I could sit around all day and talk about Grammys and Image Awards and all the honors this world can give, but that's not the main thing. Of course, I know there's a sense of accomplishment in having your peers and the public recognize what you've worked so hard to achieve. But that's just so much junk if your head's screwed up.

The world is only too ready to screw your head up, and if you think about it, that's its main objective. I often think that the secular world, the popular media, and the music crowds have been designed by the enemy to destroy the body of Christ.

The forces of evil can't stand the presence of good. If you get eight boys together and one of them is clean-cut and doesn't mess around, the other seven will start working on him until he finally gives in and starts acting just like them. That's how the enemy works.

In my own case, I was wrestling with all kinds of

emotions during those growing-up years. Not just promiscuity, but I was different; and I mean *different!* I was the kind of kid who would crawl up on the roof at night, look up at the stars, and just start crying. You know, a strange kind of kid.

Sometimes I'd wake up in the middle of the night and stare out the window for hours, watching the stars and the clouds pass by. I'd watch the way the light would change when the clouds would pass in front of the moon, wondering what it was all about. Other times I'd get up and go across to the living room and just play my heart out on the piano.

Now, we lived in a very small house, and even if I played softly, the noise of the piano carried all over the house. My room was up in the front, near the living room, and right across the hall from the kitchen, so it wasn't as bad as it might have been. If I couldn't sleep I'd just get up and go in there and play for two or three hours at a time or until Gertrude would finally come down and stop me. I was strange that way.

STRANGE ENCOUNTERS

I also remember seeing some other strange stuff at night. You may not believe this, but I'm convinced that what I'm about to tell you is true. I believe it happened just this way. Gertrude had a washer and dryer in the kitchen, and I remember that I always used to see—not just once but all the time—a little boy who would come out of the dryer in our kitchen and come in to see me.

Church Boy

He was like a little ghost child. He would come out of the dryer and walk up to my bed. He was my size, just a little boy, but he had no face. It was just this ghostlike image that would come over to where I was sleeping and look at me. This happened many, many times.

I've thought about that for years, and I don't have the slightest idea what it was, except that I feel it was something spiritual. I guess it may have been some sign of God's protection over me, or an angel maybe. I don't know. It never did anything to me, never said anything, but I can tell you, it used to scare me.

Anyway, I was always a strange kid. I remember going out into the back yard and staring up into the night sky. I'd sit on the roof or the back porch steps and just sing or make up little verses or talk to myself about what was going on in my life. I was a strange kid, always living in a fairy tale.

My wife, Tammy, tells me that was the poet in me trying to come out. Maybe it was. But it doesn't make me feel any better to know that. I was never content, never very secure, and I was never well liked by the other kids when I was growing up.

I was the little kid who always gave the speeches. I was the one who got to give the Christmas address. I played the piano for programs, and all the adults would smile and applaud for me. But I think that's one of the main reasons most of the kids hated me.

On the inside, I think I was always looking for something bigger. I knew there had to be something out there, something I was supposed to do, something I had to get hold of. Whether it was the effect of childhood loneliness, having a musical background, or just my unusual upbringing, there was something always lurking there and making life hard for me.

Was it the poet in me? I don't know.

Somebody suggested recently that maybe God was shaping me as a musician by putting pressures on me that would force me into the mold He had already designed for me. If I had been the best looking or the most popular guy in class, and if every time I walked into a room the whole place lit up, then maybe I wouldn't be here today. Maybe I'd be back someplace in West Fort Worth, hanging out in crack houses, or maybe I'd be down at the county jail right now. Who knows?

It has been my experience that God never shapes me through pleasure; He only seems to shape me through pain and sorrow. I don't necessarily like the way He does that; maybe I'll get a chance to ask Him about that someday. But He doesn't ask for my opinion on the matter!

I truly believe that I wouldn't have learned any of the stuff God had for me if my early life had been any easier. In that sense, I'm glad it happened the way it did, but I am also glad the hard times didn't last forever!

Let me touch You and see if You are real;
Even though I know in my heart Your hands can heal,
But sometimes I get discouraged,
And I need Your strength and shield, Jesus.
Let me touch You and see if You are real.

Sometimes to me You seem so far away,
And I wonder how to make it through the day.
But if I can touch the hem of Your garment,
Your power, I know, You can heal, Jesus.
Let me touch You and see if You are real.

When I'm down, let me touch You.
When I'm lonely, let me touch You.
When I'm discouraged, let me touch You.
Like I never have before.
Lord, I need You more and more, Jesus.
Let me touch You and see if You are real.

Words and music by Kirk Franklin.
Copyright © 1995, Kerrion Publishing / Lilly Mack Publishing (BMI).
Used by permission.

3

Let Me Touch You

I've always had an active imagination, and I've always had a million things going on inside my head at the same time. When I was in school, I used to let my imagination run away with me at times. I know I should have paid more attention to what my teachers were saying—my grades prove that!—but I was constantly thinking about other things, other ideas, and I was spending a lot more time wondering about crazy stuff than I was focusing on the subject at hand.

I remember times when I would be sitting there talking to somebody, and suddenly I'd realize my thoughts were a thousand miles away. Just thinking about something ordinary could set my mind in a spin, and before long I'd be wondering about problems I had never even had or imagining places I'd probably never see.

In some ways I'm glad I'm wired that way, because some of the things I'd be thinking about were fascinating. Still, it didn't help me make very good grades in school.

But that way of thinking—living in a world of imagination—has always been a big part of who I am. Even now, when I'm performing onstage with the Family, I do a lot of improvisation. Sometimes we'll be performing a number we've done hundreds of times and, just on the spur of the moment, I'll change the words of the song and the Family will follow along with me. If I change them another way, they follow me that way too.

They know me! They know what I'm like. I think they're always ready for the unexpected. One of our lead singers tells me all the time that I'm skating on that fine line between genius and insanity, and maybe he's right! I prefer to think of it as being inspired!

I also realize now that those escape runs into the world of the imagination were, at least in some ways, a kind of defense mechanism. Life was pretty hard when I was growing up, and the pressures of school, my peer group, and my responsibilities at church sometimes seemed like more than I could handle. So that fantasy world was my only refuge, and it became my mental hideout.

Even when I try to think about those times now, I find it uncomfortable. It's amazing how much I have forgotten about my early life. Most people remember a lot more about their childhood than I do, but I think the reason I let so much of it slip my mind is life was so complicated and painful. Even today there are things I don't want to know about, and I'd prefer not to remember some of the stuff that happened to me then.

First of all, I wasn't popular with the other kids, so I was always trying extra hard to make them like me. When I tell you I was always trying to be liked, I'm not kidding! But the more I tried, the less they liked me.

I remember my first grade teacher whipping me in class, right in front of all the other children. I cried like a baby while all the other kids just laughed, and there was nobody to complain to. There was nobody to take up for me or tell me that things would get better.

Some people today find that hard to believe, but back in the seventies, parents in our neighborhood would say to the teacher, "If that boy of mine gives you any trouble in school, you have my permission to whip his behind!" I don't think they can do that anymore, but in the seventies it wasn't uncommon at all—at least, not in all-black schools. And I'm pretty sure Gertrude agreed with that philosophy. She wanted me to do right, and she didn't spare the rod.

So I was teased a lot. Most of the time, the little girls I thought were cute wouldn't give me the time of day. When I was in the first grade I was blown away by this one girl, and she didn't even know I existed. She was the smartest girl in our class—I thought she was brilliant because she was the first one to learn how to write in cursive. But I was just a clown in her book, and that made me feel pretty bad about myself.

OUTSIDE LOOKING IN

Practically every girl I ever liked in school did not like me. And, unfortunately, the girls who liked me, I didn't especially like—at least not for girlfriends. But there was one girl I really liked in second grade. Her name was Tanya, and I can still remember what she looked like. For a couple of days I thought Tanya was going to be my special friend, but it never did work out. And I remember when the whole thing fell through.

We were learning to tell time. Tanya's desk was close to mine, and we were both doing pretty well, learning the hours and minutes on the clock. The teacher would move the hands around on this big cardboard clock at the front of the room, then she'd ask each of us to tell what time it was.

I could usually give the right answer if the hands were either straight up on the hour or on the half hour, so when it was my turn I could tell her if it was five o'clock or six-thirty or something like that. All that first day I was giving the right answers. The kids were giving me applause, and I was feeling pretty good about it. Whenever I'd look around, I could see that Tanya was liking me, and that was really cool.

But the next day we started doing the quarter hours, and this time I didn't have a clue. Man, they laughed at me! I'd give the wrong answer time after time, and Tanya was so embarrassed she said, "Kirk Franklin, you're just stupid!" I mean, I went from hero to zero in two days' time!

I bring that up because that's how a lot of my childhood was. When I was playing the piano and making music I was the hero, but when I was doing anything else I was the clown. In my memory that seems to be the best image I can think of for my whole growing-up experience.

Gertrude's husband, Jack, had relatives who lived down the street and around the corner from us. You would think it would have been nice to have family nearby, but that wasn't really the case. Now remember, I was adopted, so I wasn't really a Franklin, and all these cousins and kin-folk let me know it in no uncertain terms.

Their attitude was, "You're not family, and you don't belong here!"

I tried to act as if I didn't care, but you know how those words hurt me. I always seemed to be on the outside look-ing in.

Jack's sister had grandchildren who were about my age, and next door to them lived a bunch of cousins who were also about the same age. Across the street there were kids our age, and there were others who'd come over to play. There must have been fifteen or twenty kids in that group, but I was the one they all decided to laugh at and pick on.

I'm sorry to say, it wasn't just the kids who gave me a hard time; even their parents joined in. I could come around the corner and the grownups would make their chil-dren go inside the house because they thought I was bad.

I wasn't bad. I was just weird! I was just so excited about the idea of playing with other kids that most of the time I would overplay. It's like the kids who get the ball and want to make every shot. I didn't get to play with kids very often, and I was starved for it. So when I got to be with kids my age I just went crazy. But that made the other kids (and their parents) think I was some kind of weirdo. And maybe I was!

When Gertrude would go to keep house for the white family I mentioned earlier, she would usually take me along. She didn't want me underfoot while she was working, though, so she'd drop me off at a recreational complex called the Bethlehem Center. It was like a YMCA, run by the city.

I was small and puny, and I'd been raised by an old woman, so I didn't really fit in with most of that crowd, and I didn't know how to play. Most of the boys were hard and tough. They knew how to fight, and they could spit and curse and do stuff like that. So whenever we would play football or basketball or soccer, I'd get killed. And whenever we played indoor games, they didn't want anything to do with me because I was too little.

There was just one thing I could do that was outstanding, one thing that made me stand out in a good way. I could play the piano. People always liked me when they found out I could play the piano. The girls liked me, and they would hang around with me when they discovered I could play.

So, as you might imagine, it didn't take me long to realize this could be a good thing, and I learned to take advantage of my talent. I'll never forget one particular day, during recess, when I went into the room where the piano was and I started playing. I wasn't showing off or trying to impress anybody at first. I just saw the piano and felt like playing.

Well, before I knew it, all the kids started coming in from all over the place. They said, "Oh, Kirk Franklin, you can really play the piano!"

Then somebody yelled, "Hey, Kirk, can you play 'Stayin' Alive'?"

So I started playing all the hot seventies songs. I was

just playing along, laughing and having a great time, and it turned into this big party. Before it was over, I had turned the whole recreation center into a big concert. I'll never forget that.

I was probably about seven years old at that time, and I had the place going wild. At last, a moment of glory! It was so refreshing not to be the butt of everybody's jokes for a change. That day stands out as one of my fondest memories of those early years.

RAINY DAYS

By the time I got to the fourth grade, I was going through some major changes in my life. In one case, what should have been a blessing turned out to be a nightmare. Thanks to some crazy computer glitch, or maybe due to some teacher's totally misguided recommendation, I accidentally wound up in the magnet-school program in Fort Worth.

If you're not familiar with the magnet-school concept, then you should know that magnet schools are special schools for kids with special academic qualifications. Boys and girls are brought together from all over the community to participate in accelerated programs of various kinds. Magnet schools were really coming on strong back in the late seventies, and I think there are still quite a few of them around today.

So the city of Fort Worth had started a magnet-school program in our area, at Eastern Hills Elementary, and however it happened, I got a letter saying I had been accepted as a student in this new program.

Gertrude and I didn't know what to think. It seemed like an honor, but there was absolutely no evidence in my record to suggest that I was that bright. I didn't perform well academically. Besides, I hadn't applied for admission and didn't know anybody who might have recommended me, so it was strange.

As I said earlier, I was always doing something else, like day-dreaming, when the other kids were working on their lessons. Most of the time my head was in outer space or somewhere else, and I was either drawing or playing games or acting crazy, because my mind was so active and I thought school was so incredibly boring.

Despite our doubts and concerns, the school district decided I would have to go to this magnet-school program — and I absolutely hated it.

First of all, I hated moving from one school to another. I had to be bused to the new school, and that was no fun. But, as I suspected, it didn't take them long to realize they had made some kind of technical error. I wasn't supposed to be there!

Sometime during the second six weeks the principal called and asked Gertrude to come up to the school. We all got together with my teachers, and they said my grades weren't up to the standards of the school. As far as I know I was the only kid this happened to, but I was sure it was some kind of computer mistake.

So there I was, at a school where I knew I didn't

belong. Rather than embarrass me, they decided to let me stay the rest of the year, but it was a strange time. I remember at one point we had to write limericks in English class. This was in the fourth grade, and the reason I remember it so vividly was because of the reaction of the teacher.

My limerick wasn't like the others. It wasn't funny like most of them. It said:

There once was a kid named Kirk;
The kids all called him a jerk.
When he went out to play,
It turned into a rainy day.
That goofy little kid named Kirk.

I realize now what a sad statement that was, but that was how I was feeling at the time. My teacher was surprised when I read my verse, and I don't know whether she was angry or shocked. But she looked at me very strangely. Maybe she realized I was a sensitive child, or maybe she saw that I had a poetic nature. She probably just thought I was goofy!

Either way, I suspected that everybody in the class, including the teacher, knew I didn't belong there, because I was always so far behind the rest of the class.

I was always challenged and embarrassed, and I felt the pressure more, I think, because I was the only black boy in the whole class. I don't know why, but I always seemed to wind up in situations where I was the only little black boy in a sea of white faces.

With my grown-up eyes I can see now that there's a hurting child inside the poem I wrote; but when I read it out loud that day, most of the kids just laughed at me. I didn't think much about it until later, but I realize now what a cry for love it was.

Now, at Eastern Hills Elementary, the whole school wasn't a magnet school. They had a magnet program, but they had regular classes too. So, even though I was the only black kid in that particular class, there were black children in the regular classes.

And I remember that there was one particular teacher who made a real impression on me—Mrs. Barnett. She was the only black teacher I had any contact with at the school, and she was really on it! I thought she was the bomb! I mean, I was impressed with everything she did. She talked as well as any of the white teachers, she was smart, and she just sounded good. I was really glad she was there.

Mrs. Barnett helped me, and she gave me a chance to get involved. They had a black history program at this school, and she asked if I'd like to give the Martin Luther King speech that year.

Now, if you've heard it or read it, you know it's a long speech, so I was reluctant to try it at first. But Mrs. Barnett encouraged me. She assured me I could do it, and she took her time with me to help me learn the words all the way through. On three or four occasions, she even took me home with her after school to give me extra time to practice. I'll never forget that. She really focused me.

Church Boy

It's fascinating when I think about it now, how that one teacher would take the time to do something special for a kid like me. I mean, there I was, knowing I was in the wrong school, with the wrong people, doing the wrong stuff, and this woman took time from her busy schedule for me—to encourage me, to teach me, and to help me do something I could be proud of. It was a blessing I'll never forget.

I remember getting up in front of the whole school that day, and I really got into the part. I had seen Dr. King give that speech on TV when I watched the special about his assassination, so I knew what it was supposed to sound like. I went up to the microphone and recited the whole thing with as much expression as I could give it:

Even though we face the difficulties of today and tomorrow, I still have a dream. It is a dream deeply rooted in the American dream. I have a dream that one day this nation will rise up, live out the true meaning of its creed: "We hold these truths to be self-evident, that all men are created equal." I have a dream that one day on the red hills of Georgia, the sons of former slaves and the sons of former slave-owners will be able to sit down together at the table of brotherhood. I have a dream.

That's just part of it, of course; I memorized the whole speech, and I still remember it to this day. My grandkids will probably have to listen to me recite it thirty years from now! They won't be able to escape it!

Obviously, that experience made a big impression on me. It's such an important speech, especially for African Americans and especially during black history week. I had been selected to stand up in front of the whole school to give this important address, and that was the one meaningful thing I got to do while I was at that school.

I had never wanted to be an actor, but I got to be one that day. I didn't have to read the words, because I knew them by heart. And I tried to express the same passion and emotion that Dr. King had felt, standing there on the Capitol Mall in Washington, D.C. I said it just the way I had heard him say it. I felt those words in my soul.

I'm certain that the school district would have let me stay at the magnet school if my academics had come up, but of course they didn't. So the next year, for the fifth grade, I had to go back to my old school.

MAKING SENSE OF IT ALL

What impact did that year have on me? Was it a good experience, being transferred back and forth like that? Did I gain from it? Yes. I would have to say I gained, even though it was painful for me, because I got a glimpse of a different world; and, for the first time, I saw how the other half lives. I'm glad I did.

The emotional stress I went through during all of that, however, reminds me of something I read recently that said the emotional pressures that turn some people into geniuses are the very same ones that drive other people nuts. Well, I can't swear that's true, but the idea sure makes sense to me!

When I think about some of the pressures I was living with when I was growing up, I'm amazed I ever survived. But I don't have any bitterness about my childhood. I'm just glad I did survive, and I'm glad that somehow God used those things to make me stronger. I stumbled and fell more times than I can count. But I'm still standing, and I feel that I've been blessed in a very special way.

Someone told me not too long ago that being an outsider—being ridiculed and made fun of like I was—may have been the thing that drove me to express my musical talents as I have the past several years. They said that if God had not allowed all those pressures and rejections, I might not have written the songs or had the blessings or Godly success I've enjoyed lately.

Even if that's true, it doesn't make the memories any easier or take away the sting of those old pains. We tend to think our experiences are unique when they happen, and we think that what we're doing is just part of some natural evolution. We don't think very much about the big picture.

But I'm pretty sure, in either case, that I would never volunteer to go back through those things again, even if I knew they might help me achieve some level of Godly success later in life. It's definitely not worth it!

But even in the hardest of times, when I was ten and eleven years old, a lot of people were beginning to say that I was probably going to be involved in music when I grew up. By eleven years old, I was leading the church choir at Mount Rose Baptist Church, and in hindsight, I suppose that is pretty remarkable—though it didn't seem very remarkable at the time.

There were two sides to that story too. On one hand, it wasn't easy getting the older adults even to let an eleven-year-old kid tell them how to sing or what to sing. They complained loudly until somebody finally said, "Hey, you know, the kid's pretty good!" I suppose that should have told me there was something going on—that maybe I did have a gift God could use—but I didn't see that at the time.

As I think about it now, I can almost imagine God looking down at this little kid and saying, "Now, how in the world am I going to channel this strange little boy so he'll wind up going with his heart instead of his emotions? How can I teach him to love and not to hate?"

He may have said, "One way I can do that is to give him a hard life so people won't like him—so he'll have to look a little deeper for the meaning of things—and so he'll have to turn to Me for help and guidance."

Is that just my imagination again? Maybe. But maybe not.

I would soon find out that there were times still ahead that would be even harder than what I had experienced up to that point. If I thought things had been tough in grade school, by the time I got to junior high school I found out I hadn't seen anything yet. Now *that* was a challenge!

That's when I met Marcus. For whatever reason, Marcus and I started hanging together, doing things, and for the first time I began to think that maybe I could have a friend in life. For the first time, I had me some homies who weren't bashing me all the time and giving me a hard time about being "Church Boy."

Marcus knew about stuff I only dreamed about, things like being a player, being liked by the girls, and being popular. I was so excited about going into junior high, I can still remember everything I was wearing the first day of school. But for all my expectations and optimism, it was a culture shock.

Except for that one disappointing semester at Eastern Hills magnet school, I had been in all-black schools all my life, so there was nothing about the culture I was going into that was new to me. But I had never seen anything like the older kids in junior high. I had never been in schools where the boys were so hard, so cool, and so together. At least, that's how it seemed to my young eyes.

These kids were in the seventh and eighth grade, just one or two grades above me, but they were so far ahead of me in everything else that I was hypnotized by everything they did.

Then I met Marcus, and I sort of inherited a whole network of friends. Marcus not only had friends in the junior high, he had friends and uncles in the high school just down the street. He knew people, and he knew the game. He was very popular, but for some unknown reason he and I hooked up. Suddenly I had some juice.

We would go up to the high school every day after school. We had to go up there to catch the city bus to go home. I felt like I was on another planet, but Marcus knew people at the high school and had seen things I didn't know about. He knew how to be cool, and I was impressed with that.

But one day when Marcus was joking around with me he grabbed my jacket and threw it in some water. All the older guys were laughing at me, and once again I was just this little kid. I was surprised and hurt. I couldn't say anything or do anything about it, so I just walked away crying. I thought that was the end of our friendship and that Marcus had just been making a joke of me all along.

But somehow he got my phone number, and later that night he called my house and apologized. He could see that I had been hurt by what happened, and after that he let me start hanging around with him and his friends. Now understand, Marcus and I were in the same grade, we were both sixth-graders, but he was way cooler than I could ever hope to be. He'd been around. He knew how to talk about sex. He knew all the curse words.

The next person who made a big impression on me at that time was a guy named Stacy. Stacy lived in our neighborhood, and I guess I should probably have met him before I met Marcus, because he lived closer. But Stacy lived across the tracks. My house was in a neighborhood called Riverside, and, believe it or not, the train tracks ran right down through the middle of town.

It's like you hear about, like something out of an old movie. One side of the tracks was horrible, and the other side was better. I lived on the side that was better, and the reason was I lived in a neighborhood with a lot more older people. It wasn't better from an economic standpoint necessarily, but people where I lived were older and more settled.

But all the cool guys hung out on the other side of the tracks. They were tough. They all knew how to drink and fight, and they smoked weed. Well, one night Stacy spent the night at my house, and he knew some guys, so we went out and got some weed. That was the sixth grade, remember, and I was only about eleven years old at the time. We smoked a joint, and it was my initiation into the big league.

BREAKING OUT

So I started hanging with Marcus and Stacy. Now, remember, I had been raised by an old woman who wanted to keep me in short pants and make me her little baby—the baby she never had—but I was about ready to bust out. So Marcus and Stacy taught me about being a player, and that's when things started to change.

They kept talking about this place they liked to go called Jolly Time. Jolly Time was a popular skating rink, but it was not your average skating rink. It was a place where you could skate until about nine or ten, and after that everybody would take off their skates and go out to the middle of the floor and dance.

So it was like a skating rink/nightclub. And it was on the rough side of Fort Worth, a place called Stop Six, so called because that's where the number six city bus would stop. And there were all kinds of tough guys and gangsters hanging out over there.

I'll never forget how excited I was when Gertrude finally let me go with Marcus and Stacy to Jolly Time. Before all this, mind you, I was Church Boy. But after months of begging and pestering, she finally agreed to let me go, and that would bring about some big changes in my life.

Seeing girls! Older girls dancing! I mean, this was stuff the Sunday school teachers had been telling me about, and I wasn't supposed to be seeing this stuff. But it was off the hook!

By this time I was playing piano for the church, not to mention occasional music jobs and performances at other places. I was a fairly regular musician on the weekends, and people in the black churches around Fort Worth were getting to know who I was.

Gertrude was the one who kept track of all that. She wasn't a promoter at all, and she was not a stage mother like you hear about. She just made the decisions about when and where I could play, and if anybody wanted us to do a special concert or an Easter program or something like that, they had to go through her.

Thanks to my job at Mount Rose Baptist Church, I was making a hundred dollars a month, so I always had some pocket change. A hundred dollars a month may not seem like much now, and for a grownup it wasn't much even then. But for a sixth-grader, that was some serious cheddar! And to me it felt like a fortune.

Church Boy

Normally, Gertrude was very careful about where I went and who I went with. She believed that my musical talents were a gift from God, and she tried to guide me so I would always be available for the Lord's service.

She never saw my musical ability as a way to make money. She had already turned down a recording contract with a gospel music label when I was seven years old because she didn't think it was right for me at that time. She didn't think I was ready emotionally or spiritually for a recording contract. She was very spiritual, and I trusted her judgment. I was upset, but now I know for a fact that she was right.

But the allure and the appeal of hanging out with a flashy, worldly, popular crowd was more than I could resist. I had been so unpopular up to that time that I was starved for attention.

I'll never forget that first night at Jolly Time. I was dressed preppier than everybody else. I was all button-down, and I was looking good! I had on my cool slacks while everybody else had on blue jeans and baseball caps. Besides, I came in with Stacy and Marcus, and everybody knew they were cool. They were into sports. I wasn't in sports at that time, but I was hanging with these two dudes who were popular and well known, and I was totally caught up in the glow.

But that night, after all the skating and dancing and being cool and popular, I came home about one or two o'clock in the morning, and Gertrude was furious! She let me know what I was doing, and what God thought about late-night carousing and every kind of vice that comes from going to the clubs, and she really made it sting.

So, do you think I stopped right there and realized the error of my ways?

No, of course not. I wish I had seen the truth of her words at that time, but I didn't. I was too young, too immature, and I was totally caught up in the glamour of what was going on out there. I had had one taste of a fast, exciting, wild, different kind of life, and I wanted more.

From that moment on, my relationship with Gertrude started to change. From that moment on, our relationship started going downhill.

Gertrude was a spiritual woman. She was very, very serious about her faith. When she could see that I was following these wild young kids and that I had that twinkle of the world in my eyes, she must have thought, *I've lost my baby.*

I know she cried over me, and she would have plenty of reason to cry over the next few years. But at the same time, I don't think she was prepared for the idea of seeing her baby grow up. I think the distance that came between us, changing our relationship, was a combination of those two things.

A little while later, when girls started calling the house to talk to me, she was very upset with me. She didn't like me talking on the phone with girls all the time. She didn't think it was proper. Even if they called late in the evening when I wouldn't be tying up the phone, she would be very upset with me. I thought I was just being a typical, seventies-style boy.

Little by little, I started retaliating against her, upset at what seemed to be her lack of sensitivity to my youth and my need to grow up. I started talking back and doing things that were designed to drive Gertrude into a rage.

I said earlier that today I'm a rebel with a cause, but in those days I was a rebel without a cause. I just wanted to grow up, and I was going to get a taste of what the world had to offer. I mean, here was my chance to be cool, and I was sick and tired of being looked at like this little punk Church Boy.

I wasn't involved in sports. Most of the kids I knew had been raised in sports, but I wasn't even exposed to them. Some of my friends were in Pee Wee Football or playing at the Boy's Clubs or the YMCA. But when did I have time to do any of that? For me it was either Vacation Bible School or youth choir or practicing for holiday musicals. I didn't have either the time or the opportunity to get into sports, and I missed all that. Marcus and Stacy were athletes, however, and they had taken me under their wing.

INSULT ON TOP OF INJURY

So that's how my life had been going. But when I was in the seventh grade, something changed. My biological mother married a guy named Charles, and suddenly I thought I saw a faint ray of hope.

Things were getting harder all the time with Gertrude. She was being "old school" and I wasn't; our relationship was going south. When I found out Deborah was about to get married, I thought maybe I would have a real daddy after all. Maybe this would be my chance to have a real family who would help me and be more understanding of my need to stretch.

I had never lived with Deborah, but I knew she was my birth mother. So this new marriage looked like the answer I had been hoping for. Maybe it would be my big chance.

I've always been a pleaser, so at first I wanted to dress like Charles. If he would come over in overalls, then I'd want to put on overalls. If he had on a sweater or a jacket, then I'd go put on my sweater or my jacket so I could look like Charles. Obviously, I needed a male role model in my life, and I needed a daddy to look up to. I never had that, and I was soon to find out that Charles wasn't going to be my dream come true either.

In the seventh grade, all the things that had started the year before sort of blew up. I started dressing, trying to be cool, smoking weed, drinking beer, getting into fights, and looking for whatever else I could get into.

I mean, I had been understudy to these two cool guys for at least a year already, and I decided I could be cool on my own. I still wasn't popular, and I wasn't liked by the girls all that much, so I decided to go out for the football team.

Other things were happening too. By this time I was

driving everybody crazy, so Gertrude and Deborah both asked Charles to do something about it, to get involved in my life. Unfortunately, he wasn't involved consistently. So this wasn't the best thing that could have happened for me at the time. Before long, it became pretty clear that Charles wasn't going to be the role model I was hoping for.

This became painfully clear one day when I was getting ready for a football game. Charles came up there and found me out on the field after school. Without saying a word, he grabbed me by the shoulder, dragged me to the car, and shoved me inside.

Then, while I was still shaking my head, trying to figure out what was up, he reached over and popped me in the chest with his fist and said, "You been wasting your time in school, young Mr. Franklin, getting yourself in trouble, making bad grades, and driving your mother crazy. You been giving us all kinds of trouble, and it's about time somebody settled you down."

Then he drove me home to his house. I didn't know what to expect, but I wasn't saying much.

Remember how you used to get those three-week and six-week progress reports in school? Well, I got a bad progress report that term, and apparently that's why Charles was hot. Deborah had told him I'd been goofing around, acting like a clown and causing trouble in school, and he said she had told him to discipline me and get me back on track. This was his idea of talking sense to me.

"You want to be a man?" he said, shoving me backward

and humiliating me. "Well, we'll just treat you like a man." Then he yanked off his belt and started beating me with it.

I really tried to do better the following term because I didn't want a repeat of that scene. But when the next progress reports came out, my grades were even worse. So Charles came back, grabbed me again, and took me back to his house. This time he beat the living daylights out of me.

He made me strip down to my underwear and then took off his leather belt and laid into me with everything he had, until eventually I was totally unable to resist. I'll never forget the terror, the pain, and the anger I felt. He was swinging the belt so hard that, at one point, he hit the light fixture overhead and shattered it. Glass went flying everywhere.

I knew I wasn't going to be able to get away from him, so I started acting like some glass got in my eye. Charles stopped swinging long enough to drag me to the bathroom. He got me under the light and looked in my eyes to see if there was any glass. He didn't see anything, so he splashed some water in my face then dragged me out to the living room and finished the job he had started in the garage.

But that wasn't even the worst part. Back in the early eighties, the cool thing for black kids at our school was wearing jheri curls. There's always some kind of cool hairstyle. Back in the fifties, I understand, a lot of black guys would get their hair pressed. Sammy Davis Jr. did that, and that was the bomb for a while.

Today some guys get buzz cuts or shave their heads. But in those days the cool thing was jheri curls, and I had my hair done that way. So, to make my humiliation complete, Charles took me down to the barber shop and got all my hair cut off.

That was the worst part. The beating was bad enough, but cutting my hair was an even deeper kind of pain, and he knew that. That's why he did it.

By the beginning of the seventh grade, the girls were just starting to like me a little better. I was dressing cool, I had jheri curls, and I was getting into sports. But Charles changed all that. He made me look stupid, and yanked me off the team. When I went back to school with this short, nappy-looking haircut, everybody looked at me like, "Oh yeah, he's ugly again!"

Even at church, the kids laughed at me. They made fun of my clothes, joked about Gertrude's old Chevy Impala, and called me names. Gertrude wasn't a very fashionable dresser, so some of the kids would even tease me about the way she looked. Those were trying times.

When I went to choir rehearsal, I'd have to ride the bus, so sometimes I showed up late, sweaty, and really embarrassed. Even though I'd worshiped in that community all my life, there were times when I felt like an outsider.

The other kids had big brothers and sisters or sometimes parents to take them around and look after them. But I was on my own most of the time, and I was taking a beating, not just in school but also from the kids at church!

So all these things were piling up on me, and I was getting in more and more trouble, until one day Gertrude said, "Kirk, I've had enough. I can't deal with you anymore. I want you to go live with Deborah."

SEEDS OF DISAPPOINTMENT

Deborah had been through lots of boyfriends and live-ins in her life, but she had never been married before. Now that Charles was there, there was somebody around who was more than willing to give me a little discipline, even if it killed me. Gertrude thought that was a good way to solve our problems. At least, she never tried to stop it.

She called Charles and told him what she was thinking, and Charles said that would be okay. He drove over and picked me up. But this time I had mixed feelings about the whole idea of living with him and Deborah.

I knew what Gertrude was thinking, and I knew Charles and Deborah weren't going to be the best parents in the world. I think part of me was still hoping that maybe this would be the chance to have the parents I'd never had. For a minute or two, it seemed like a good idea. After all, Charles had a nice house.

Most of the kids I knew had nice places to live, and most of the kids at our church had nice houses. But Gertrude and I lived in this little shack. So the idea of moving in with Charles and Deborah had some appeal.

Church Boy

But Charles had no sooner come and got me when Deborah came home from work and threw a huge fit. She said she did not want me in that house. She didn't want anything to do with me, and she said something to Gertrude that night I'll never forget. She said, "I didn't want him in the first place, and you know that! If it weren't for you I would have aborted him, but you wouldn't let me!"

What devastating words those were for me to hear. The sound of them has been etched in my mind ever since.

By the time of Gertrude's death in 1990, we were getting along okay. But our relationship was strained, and it never was as good after that as it had been when I was a little boy. I don't feel any bitterness about that time. As I get older, I can see why she was worried about me. But I also know that that old woman saved my life, and she loved me the best way she knew how. She worried about me all the time, and sometimes she made things a lot harder than they needed to be. But I know what she did, and I'll never forget that. She saved my life.

At one point I got into trouble and had to go to a school for bad kids for a while. I didn't know it at the time, but I was walking on the sheer edge of disaster. I almost flunked the seventh grade and just barely squeaked by. I tried to settle down a little in the eighth grade. I got to play football again. By that time Charles was out of the picture, so I didn't have to worry about him.

I grew my jheri curls back, and I was starting to be a little bit cool. The girls started liking me again. It really sounds funny to me now to say that a fourteen-year-old guy would have to have just the right hairstyle, but that's the way it was. None of the cool girls would date a nappy-headed guy in those days!

But the biggest change was that in the eighth grade I started hanging with a guy named Byron. He was older than I was, and he was cool. He was already out of school, but he let me hang with him. He brought me up under his wing. He was into smoking weed, and he was a real lady's man; so at that point Byron became my role model.

Best of all, Byron had a white Ford Thunderbird. It was real nice, and everybody thought his car was the joint. Nobody I knew had wheels like that. So that's the kind of company I was keeping—Marcus, Stacy, and then Byron—and through their eyes I was learning how to be cool. I'm sorry to say that it was only in hindsight that I could see I was doing all the wrong things. I was so desperate for friends, I was willing to learn from guys who were showing all the wrong stuff.

Michael Jackson was the mega-star of the day; his album *Thriller* was out, and I was getting into dancing. So now when we would go down to Jolly Time for the dances on Saturday nights, I was the guy all the girls wanted to dance with. I was dressing sharper, hanging with a faster crowd, and becoming known as a good dancer.

Marcus and Stacy had been cool, but they operated on a smaller scale. Now that I was hanging with Byron, I started moving into an older, cooler crowd. It was a dangerous time, and I never saw what was coming next.

Transitions
(Part 2)

It really doesn't matter what you're going through,
I know that Jesus can work it out for you.
His yoke is easy, and His burden's light;
Just give it to Jesus. He'll make it all right.

He can handle it;
He can handle it.

There's no doubt about my Savior; I know He will deliver.
He can handle it.

There's no doubt about my Savior,
I know He will deliver.

Whatever it is, I know He can . . .
He can handle it.
He can handle it.
He can handle it.

4

He Can Handle It

ll through junior high school, I was getting deeper and deeper into stuff that, if I had had any sense at all, I would have stayed away from. But you know how it is with teenagers. Along with all the mind games I was into because of my youth and immaturity, there was also a lot of promiscuity going on. I'm not proud of that, but I can't deny that I fell into it. The physical thorn in the flesh was always there.

I wish I had understood what I was doing at the time, but I didn't. I was a promiscuous young man; it would be dishonest to pretend it didn't happen. I did what I assumed everybody else was doing at the time. That was a very challenging time for me; my last year in junior high continued about the same as the year before — fast, hard, and crazy — except that everything started moving a lot faster as I got older.

Thanks to my interest in music, I got to know Jack Franklin's relatives who lived nearby a little better. These were the folks who had always been so hard on me ever since I was adopted. But it turned out that they were interested in music and break-dancing. One of them, a brother named Archel, said he thought we needed to get into that.

Kirk Franklin

In the early- to mid-eighties, break-dancing was really hot, and if you were pretty good at it, you could get invited to a lot of parties. So we were doing a lot of dancing, going to clubs, hanging out, and becoming a little better known.

The high school I was planning on going to the following year was just down the street from the junior high school I was attending. It was a mostly white school, and it wasn't considered to be all that cool by the kids I was hanging with. But one day Archel told me that his family was going to move several miles away to an apartment across the street from another school, O. D. Wyatt High School. It was a school with an outstanding music program, and everybody I knew said it was very cool. Besides that, it was an all-black school. So I really wanted to go there.

By that time I was into clothes, big time. I was very fashion conscious, and this school was known for that. It was a popular school with most of the guys I knew, and it was where all the cool dressers were going. So I decided that's where I needed to be. But first I had to work things out with both families so I could live with Archel during the week and then go home to Gertrude's house on weekends.

Archel and I were cool with one another. We got along fine, but his folks still treated me about the same as they had when I was a kid. They were very distant, cold, and generally suspicious of me, and they just didn't seem to like me very much. I wasn't really family. I was Gertrude's adopted boy, and they thought I was weird.

I guess it was really Archel's grandmother who didn't care much for me; but I managed to hang on, and somehow

I made it through the year without going crazy or getting myself killed. So the ninth grade was about the same for me as the eighth grade had been, only on a slightly bigger scale. Everything I'd been doing in junior high was still going on—only it was more available than before.

One good thing was that Wyatt High School had the best choir in the city. Under the direction of Jewell Kelly, the choir had won all kinds of music awards. Wyatt was known for its excellent music and fine arts departments. It had an a cappella choir, a show choir, and an outstanding music program in all areas, so I was anxious to get involved. I signed up for music classes as a freshman, and I stayed involved with music activities all through high school. I was in the choir, the band, the jazz band, drama classes, and anything else I could find that had anything to do with music.

DEEPER IN DEBT

At the same time, I was keeping my eye out for a little action, and there were a lot of fine young ladies at this school. It wasn't long before I got interested in a girl who was already a junior, two years older than I was. There I was, a fifteen-year-old freshman hanging out with this "older woman," and my friends thought that was the bomb!

My cousin lived right across the street from the high school, so we would go over there after school when everybody's parents were at work; those apartments got to be more like a motel. Now, I know that was bad news, but it seemed sweet back then. None of those people were God-fearing people. They weren't atheists, of course, but God just wasn't important to them. That fact began to play on my mind.

All through this time, I did have some kind of under-standing of spiritual things, but it was mostly just head knowledge. I knew the words, I knew what I was supposed to believe, and I knew that faith in God was important. But I wasn't living the life, and the faith I claimed to believe on the inside hadn't yet changed me on the outside.

It was the same situation I'd been fighting all my life. I was trying to beat that little punk image, always trying to get some respect and self-esteem. I was into clothes, I was into girls, and I didn't have anybody making sure I was okay.

I felt like I was just out there by myself. I didn't have anybody to ask me about my homework or to check on how I was spending my time. I didn't have anybody telling me that, as a freshman, I shouldn't be taking three elec-tives. I was taking drama, jazz band, and choir and no solid subjects.

Somebody should have told me I couldn't do that, but nobody was paying attention. They didn't warn me about any of that. In fact, when the director of the jazz band found out one semester that I wasn't signed up for his class, he went down to the counselor's office and got me transferred back into music when I should have been focusing more on academics.

I should have been hitting the books, but there I was, a freshman in high school taking three electives. The result was that I flunked the ninth grade and had to go to summer school. But, remember, this was a school that was famous for kickin' it, drinking beer, smoking weed, partying, and messing around. So, rather than doing my schoolwork, I fell in with the same easy crowd and ended up flunking summer school as well.

That only made me feel worse, and everybody really rubbed it in, telling me I was stupid or lazy or both. By the time I got to the tenth grade, I knew something had to give, and it was at that point that I started trying—in a small way at least—to get a grip on my life. It was then that things started to change inside me, and from that small beginning I started a journey, coming around to being the person I am today.

Back then I never knew what I wanted to be when I grew up. I never thought about it very much. I knew what I did, I knew what I liked, and I knew how to stay busy, but I honestly don't think I ever thought about a career at any time during those years.

The reality of my situation hit me during the summer between the ninth and tenth grades when Eric Pounds, a friend of mine, got killed. Eric used to hang around with this preacher friend of ours.

One day he was there; the next day he was dead, and his death had a life-changing impact on me. He was the first person I knew around my own age who got killed, and it was a very emotional experience.

I always had an understanding of who God is. I knew all about salvation; I knew all the words. I'd been raised in the church, so I wasn't insensitive to the things of God. But obviously something needed to change. I needed a new beginning and a genuine transformation of my heart and mind, which I had somehow avoided up to that time.

I had been drifting away from my adopted mother, little by little, ever since the sixth grade. But Gertrude didn't cut me off entirely. She was the kind of woman who, if I was sick, would take care of me. If I was hurt or in trouble, she would be there for me. But she wouldn't put up with my nonsense any other time, and she was disappointed and perhaps even threatened by my attempts to grow up too soon.

It was a stressful relationship for both of us, but I never really doubted her love. I knew she cared for me, deep down. When Eric died, Gertrude could see that I was hurting, and she was there for me. She comforted me as much as she could, and we talked about the meaning of life and death and all that. She prayed with me, talked to me, and tried to encourage me, and that was a very important step on my pathway to God.

Later that summer I started hanging out with two guys named Darrell Blair and David Mann, who were also in the choir at O. D. Wyatt. I realize now that transferring over to that school really was in the will of God because that was the first time I started meeting people more like I was—that is, people who were artistic and a little different.

This was also the first time I started meeting other people my age who were into the gospel scene, as Darrell and David were. Through their friendship and influence

Church Boy

I started becoming more sensitive to the things of the Lord.

Then one day a few weeks after Eric got killed, I got down on my knees in Gertrude's den, and I got transparent with the Lord. I asked Him to forgive me for my sins, and I asked Him to come into my life and change me. From that moment on I became aware that I had started my journey back to God. I wasn't back yet, but I had a sense of peace and forgiveness after that.

I was so excited about it that I told Darrell, David, and some of the guys about the change in my life, and they were really happy for me. That was very important because if I had said the same thing to any previous group of friends, they would have just tripped, laughing at me and calling me "Church Boy." But these brothers encouraged me and said they were happy I'd finally taken the first step.

By this time I wasn't seeing much of Marcus or Stacy anymore. We were going to different high schools, so we naturally started drifting apart, seeing each other occasionally at the mall or other places like that. I would see them at Jolly Time once in a while, but that whole scene was becoming less and less important to me as time went by.

When I got saved, the very first thing I gave up was smoking weed. Then I found out sex was wrong. You may find this hard to believe, but until I was fourteen years old I had never heard anybody come right out and say that sex outside of marriage was wrong. In fact, the first time I remember anybody talking about it was on the basketball court one afternoon.

I heard some guys talking about sex, and somebody said that having sex outside of marriage was wrong and that it was a sin. That happened when I was fourteen years old, and it surprised me. Later, after I was saved, those words started working on my conscience.

GROWING PAINS

I felt guilty for all the stuff I had been into, but now I knew it was actually a sin. I needed to talk to somebody about what I had done, so I went in to see the pastor at the church I was attending.

I said, "Pastor, I just found out that sex is wrong, and I'm feeling bad about the stuff I've been doing. I'm having a hard time with it, and I don't know what to do."

His response hit me like a ton of bricks. He took a long drag on his big cigar, then as he blew out a cloud of smoke, he said, "You're young, boy. You'll grow out of it."

That was it. That was his entire sermon on the subject. No big deal; I'd get over it. Suddenly I realized it was this attitude of casual acceptance that allowed the sin to continue in some of the church community. It was this attitude that sex outside marriage was no big deal, that it was something you could adapt to in time; that was the real problem. Unfortunately, I never did grow out of it. Seeing his attitude only made it easier for me to grow into it.

Church Boy

I truly wanted to grow deeper in the faith, but those who should have been my spiritual leaders were acting as if sexual sin were no big deal. The words of that pastor were some of the most destructive words any Christian leader could have spoken to a boy my age.

To say to a young man who had already lost his virginity that sex outside of marriage was no big deal or to say that any thought he might be having about cleaning up his life and getting right with Jesus was nothing but a whim or a fantasy, that was shocking. And he was the pastor of my church!

The result was that, after I found out how to rationalize my sin, I just kept doing what I had been doing all along. And even though I was feeling guilty in ways I never had before, I became more and more promiscuous, and I did things I will always regret. After that, I knew that what I was doing was wrong, but I didn't change my behavior right away; I just felt guilty about it. My dialogue changed. My attitudes changed. But my behavior stayed the same.

By this time, in 1984 and 1985, there was a lot of interest in local gospel groups, so as Darrell, David, and I continued our interest in gospel music, I started getting involved in some of the groups in our area. Most of them weren't very sophisticated musically, but we had a good sound and our performance style worked well for churches and youth programs and things like that. We weren't trying to make a living out of it.

When I'd get involved, usually I would play keyboards

and sing. And during this time I was getting a lot of experience doing arrangements and sometimes rearrangements. We would sing Christian songs, traditional church songs, and gospel music, and little by little I started doing more of my own compositions for special programs and concerts. But all this time I was still walking on both sides of the street.

Gertrude and I were barely talking to each other, but she had put me in the Lord's hands. "Boy," she'd say, "I don't know what to do with you anymore, so I'm putting you in the Lord's hands." It sounded like a resignation, but it was probably the best thing she could have done.

It was during this time, with all these conflicting emotions knocking around inside my head, that I met the girl who would have my son. I was in the tenth grade at the time. Now that I look back on it, I think that a part of the attraction was that she reminded me of my biological mother. They were both the kind of women I wanted to love, but they didn't love me back—neither of them. I'm not saying every flaw in our relationship was her fault. It takes two to make a relationship work. I had faults also.

Satan is always looking for a place to plant his evil seeds, but he found a place in our relationship where he could harvest a garden. So I tolerated the head games and the disappointments simply because I found somebody who wanted to be as intimate as I did.

We were just two kids searching, trying to get from each other what we wanted to get from our parents. We wanted love, acceptance, and understanding, but we settled for sex. That's what got us into trouble. I didn't even have a clue then about being responsible, and I paid the price for it by getting that young woman pregnant.

I was eighteen years old when my son, Kerrion, was born. He and I are very close today, and I love my son very much; but I wish it could have happened a different way. But yet, I am very grateful; very grateful!!

I didn't have a car. Most of the time I had to take the bus to go anyplace. I didn't have an apartment of my own or anything else that belonged to me, but here was a girl who was popular and available. She would go out with me, and we would do stuff together. But it turned out to be a very painful journey. We were both good people but bad for each other. We simply brought out the worse in each other because of the luggage from our childhood.

By the time I got to the eleventh grade, I was feeling that I didn't have anyplace to belong anymore. I wasn't doing very well in school, and I was making lousy grades. I had flunked the ninth grade, and on top of everything else, some of the kids started teasing me about being weird; somebody even started a rumor that I was gay. So all of a sudden I had a whole new battle to fight.

STICKS AND STONES

Jack Franklin's death from cancer was hard on Gertrude, but she took it in stride. When I was in the seventh grade she got remarried. I was thirteen, and Gertrude and her new husband were in their mid-seventies. Gertrude and I had been drifting apart little by little ever since I was twelve years old, but her new husband, Josh Clayborn, helped her to see that a lot of what I was going through was simply because I was a boy.

Josh had sons and grandsons from his first marriage, so he became the happy medium between Gertrude and me. I admit that at first it was very hard for me to accept him as a new influence in my life. For most of those years it had just been Gertrude and me. But now her first loyalty was to her new husband, and I felt I was just the boy she was raising.

That really hit home one day when I happened to see them kissing. I couldn't handle it! I mean, for me to go around kissing any girl I could get my hands on was one thing. But for Gertrude, who was seventy-two years old by that time, and Josh, an old man who was probably three years older than she was, I thought that was horrible! I mean, have you ever seen a seventy-two-year-old woman kiss a seventy-five-year-old man? It ain't a pretty sight, especially when you're fifteen.

This was also during the time that Deborah's husband, Charles, was whipping me. All my relationships were already strained on all sides. But after the wedding, I went home with Deborah and Charles instead of going back to Gertrude's house. They needed some time for their honeymoon.

That night Deborah and Charles got into a fight, and it was so bad that he drove me home early the next morning. So I came back home early, and the next morning—smart aleck that I was—I asked Gertrude if they did it. She said,

Church Boy

"You better believe we did it!" And that just grossed me out. I could not get over it! I couldn't accept the idea of those two making love!

But despite the adjustments and the jarring experiences of new relationships, Josh became a friend to me. Gertrude still ran the house where I was involved, but Josh helped take the edge off of her defensiveness toward me, and that was good.

In every other way, though, it was still a very hard time. I was in emotional chaos. My life was a constant trial, and I hated every minute of it. I'd lie in bed at night crying my heart out because I didn't want to go to school. Now and then Gertrude would come in and sit down beside me, pat me on the head, and tell me that everything was going to be all right. She could see what was happening inside me, but she wasn't always able to stop the pain.

I think the main reason people started saying that I was gay was that I had the reputation of being "Church Boy." A lot of other kids had grown up in the church like I had, but they still acted as if church kids were weird. Christian kids didn't fight back; they would turn the other cheek or run away from a fight. At least, that's what the other kids said. On top of that, I'd been raised by an old woman, and I wasn't tough and hard like most of the other guys in my school.

I had always been more sensitive than a lot of those people. I was into music. I was writing songs and composing lyrics, and for kids in my neighborhood that meant that I was probably gay. Where I come from, young men were supposed to be hard. They were supposed to be tough, macho, and cool. But I wasn't like that.

I didn't know how to be like that. And by that time, I had already stopped growing. I'm just under five-feet-five now, and I've been this height ever since I was fourteen years old. So that was another emotional adjustment I had to make. Everybody I knew kept on growing, and they were going off and leaving me!

Later I realized that another reason the rumor that I was gay caught on so fast was because I had been hanging out with a guy who people said was gay. He was older than I was and ran around with some friends of mine even before I met him. He had a Z-28 with a T-top, and everybody thought that was cool. He looked like he could be gay—he was effeminate—but I didn't realize he really might be. Maybe it was only natural that, when kids from school saw me hanging out with this guy, they just assumed I was gay too.

Tenth grade is hard for most people. The peer pressure is intense, and the constant preoccupation with being liked, being popular, and dressing cool makes it a hard time for any teenager. But it was especially hard on me. The effect of all this was an awareness that, even though I wasn't gay, I was definitely different. I always felt like I didn't fit in with the kids around me, but in the tenth grade it became clear to me that it was never going to change.

I began to see that I wasn't really as smooth as I thought I was, and I wasn't as good looking as I wanted to be. This was also the time I finally realized I was always going to be shorter than other people my age.

Everybody else was into sports. Everybody else was tough and could handle themselves in a fight. They all seemed so much smoother and better dressed, and they had better personalities than I did. I was just the same old kid I had always been, and that wasn't getting me anywhere.

I was still music minister at my church, still directing the musicals and playing the piano and organ on Sundays. But I also began to realize that the things I had gone through during my junior high years had affected my relationship with Gertrude. During that time, Gertrude was growing more and more distant toward me, and by the tenth grade it seemed as if there was no common ground at all between us.

Except for church and the most basic things at home, such as meals and laundry, there was little to talk about that wouldn't cause us to get into an argument. So, rather than fight about stuff, Gertrude just withdrew from me.

By that time, Deborah, my biological mother, was not even a factor in my life. Needless to say, after Charles beat me up when I was thirteen, I hadn't wanted much to do with them in any way. By the time I reached high school, they had already separated and were close to divorce.

From there, I was trying to find out who in the world I was. Marcus was in a different high school, I was living with relatives, and Gertrude and I hardly spoke to each other any more. So, any way you look at it, those years when I was fifteen and sixteen years old gave me a painful reality kick.

Kirk Franklin

TURNING TO THE LIGHT

I was a Christian by this time and had stopped smoking weed. But I still had a long way to go to get to where I needed to be in my walk with the Lord. On top of that, I was having to learn a new way of life. Before, all I thought about was having fun, hanging out, drinking beer, and meeting girls. Now I knew there was a better way, and I wanted to get in step with God, but I didn't have a lot of leadership. I wasn't really sure what to do.

So the more I changed and the less I took part in all the stuff I'd been involved in before, the more people started giving me a hard time, and they started telling everybody I was gay. Kids can be brutal, and the more it hurts the more they do it.

That might not have been so bad except that when I looked around I realized that most of the people like me—people who were into clothes, music, drama and musicals, and the arts—were all gay. So that took a little adjustment.

I got into a gospel group at this time. We called ourselves the Humble Hearts, and we played for churches and musical programs of all kinds. Everybody in the band was young. They were all like me, basically, and they weren't mature enough to realize that they were dealing with damaged goods—because that's what I was at that time.

I was seeing the young lady who would eventually have my son, but we weren't getting along either. It was a strange relationship, purely physical, and other than that we weren't really compatible. We fought a lot; we were both too much into ourselves, doing our own thing, and we didn't really know how to care for each other. That just added more stress to my life.

I tried so hard to fit in and look normal that I probably made a fool of myself in the process. There just seemed to be no relief, and I still remember that as one of the most painful times in my life.

On the surface, there wasn't all that much difference between the ninth and tenth grades. But three other things, emotional and spiritual things, came together in rapid-fire succession. I had flunked the year before, my friend Eric got killed that summer, and I gave my life to the Lord. So I was looking at the same old world but with new eyes.

More and more, music was the only place where I could find relief from the pressures that were building up inside of me. Sometimes I would go off where I could just be alone at the piano, and I would play anything that came into my head. Hymns, Sunday school choruses, folk songs, rock and roll, or things I'd just make up out of my head. Whenever I was alone at the piano, I would mess around with tunes and lyrics, working out my own ideas and emotions.

Later, during that long, hot summer, another friend was killed in an automobile accident. This time it was a girl I had dated in high school, so I wrote a song for her and performed it at the funeral.

Shortly after that I wrote another song for The Humble Hearts, using the words of Psalm 51.

The words of that psalm ring out with music. Words like, "Create in me a clean heart, O God, and renew a steadfast spirit within me. Do not cast me away from Your presence, and do not take Your Holy Spirit from me." Isn't that powerful? Studying those words, I realized David must have traveled right where I was walking.

He said, "Restore to me the joy of Your salvation, and uphold me by Your generous Spirit. Then I will teach transgressors Your ways, and sinners shall be converted to You." There's a powerful sermon in those four verses found in Psalm 51:10–13, and some good music too.

In reality, there wasn't any sort of plan to my writing at that point. It never crossed my mind that someday I would use my writing as the means for taking care of my family. And even though I loved to play and even though I had always said that I would like to be a musician if I ever got the chance, my writing and composition at that stage were pretty simple and straightforward. I was dealing with a lot of perplexing emotional and spiritual problems, so the music just seemed to be the most natural way for me to express my feelings.

The musical group I was playing with at that time, the Humble Hearts, was a local group, but we were getting a little exposure. Best of all, we were finding out what it was like to be professional performers and musicians. Going around to play at churches all over North Texas gave us a lot of practice performing praise and worship music, and I started developing a real interest in writing my own songs.

Church Boy

During one period I was into the whole charismatic scene, shouting and praising the Lord and dancing. Believe me, it was a new experience for this little old Baptist boy. Going out to perform in Full Gospel and charismatic churches introduced me to other cultures and other expressions of faith. That was an eye-opening experience and an important influence on the music I write today.

Little by little and step by step, I was growing in the faith, moving toward a career in music. I was struggling with my identity and crying out to the Lord. But I soon found out He could handle it. The Lord could overcome my trials and temptations, and I was beginning to see the light. But little did I realize what was coming next.

In the coming year, during the eleventh grade, I was in for a dramatic turn of events.

Savior, more than life to me,
You are the joy and air I breathe;
No other lover shall there be
That makes my spirit sing.
Hold me close, don't let me go;
You're the only friend I'll ever know.
That is why I love You so,
More than life to me,
More than life to me.

More, more,
I've been searchin' and You are

More, more, more,
Yes, You are.

You are more than life to me,
Yes, You are.
That is why I love you so,
More than life to me.

5

More Than Life to Me

ven though I felt like an outcast most of the time, and even though I was going through some bitter disappointments, I believe that O.D. Wyatt High School was one of the best things that ever happened to me from a musical standpoint. The music and performing arts programs were so strong that they pulled me along. They gave me a sense of purpose and an emotional center, even when everything around me seemed to be falling apart.

My teachers must have realized some of the troubles I was going through; they would just let me steal away sometimes to be alone with my music, and that was very important at the time. My academics were lousy, and I was fast on my way to ending my high school education without ever receiving a diploma, but I had the sense that I was getting a first-class music education.

Now I realize it was all God's design. He knew I wasn't going to grow up to be a rocket scientist or a CPA. That's why I wasn't spending all my time in the biology lab or the math clinic. I knew if I had any gifts at all they were in music, and the lessons I needed most had to come from my own musical experiences and soul searching. However, don't get me wrong. A good education is very important. You can't just rely on gifts.

Kirk Franklin

From the ninth through the eleventh grades, the teachers who did the most to shape my skills and interests were Jewel Kelly in music, Rudy Eastman in drama, and our band teacher, James Hamilton. All three of them spent time with me, hammering stuff into me along the way and giving me a glimpse of what it means to be sensitive to the gifts.

The person who encouraged me the most as a musician was Mrs. Kelly. She was a gifted teacher and musician who taught me a lot about composition and performance. She was hard on me and wouldn't put up with poor or sloppy work, but she helped me understand the medium of musical performance in a way I don't think I ever could have learned without her help.

By the time I got to the eleventh grade, most of my relationships were in turmoil. I had to take the city bus to school and transfer twice to get there and back. Spending time with my son's mother was painful too, but it was one of the only regular things in my life. Along with all the hassles of high school, people kept saying I was gay. Sometimes the pressures were so great that whenever I was alone, I would just break down and cry.

But, you know, there was one thing about Gertrude that stands out in my memory. She could be mad at me and could stay mad at me, but if she saw that I was hurting or sick, she'd be there to take care of me. She could kick me out of the house without a second thought if I wasn't behaving right; but if she saw that I was hurting, she'd be there.

One morning I woke up feeling so bad, so discouraged,

because the situation at school seemed hopeless. Everybody knew I had flunked and was repeating the grade. The pressures of not fitting in, of catching the bus, and of putting up with all the harassment, and all the emotional pressures of the boy-girl thing were just killing me. I was really low.

I was supposed to get up and get dressed so I could catch the bus for school, but Gertrude could see that I was down. She came over and sat down beside me and said, "Baby, if you don't want to go today, you don't have to go."

As rare as it was for her to let me take a day off like that, it was reassuring to know that Gertrude cared about what I was going through. She didn't approve of everything I was into, but she loved me. I really needed that.

AN UNEXPECTED OPPORTUNITY

It was during all this that we heard about a school for musicians and artists that had just opened up a couple of years before on the campus of Texas Wesleyan University in Fort Worth. I don't remember how we found out about it, but Gertrude made a couple of telephone calls and checked into it. She told them all about my musical background then made an appointment for us to visit the campus, where I was to be given an enrollment audition.

The Professional Youth Conservatory, or PYC, had opened its doors for the first time in January 1985 as a performing arts high school for young people who showed promise of achieving careers in the entertainment and performance industries. It offered programs in dance, theater, and music, and in addition to all the standard high school requirements, they were going to have arts classes taught by professionals from the Dallas/Fort Worth area.

Dr. Steve Schooler, the headmaster, had been involved in theater, dance, and opera for many years. He knew practically everybody in the arts community in Fort Worth. He was a teacher, former TV personality, and production director for a chain of dinner theaters in the area. The school was his idea, and he was the main one putting everything together.

He had earned a doctorate in fine arts from Texas A&M University, and he was involved in a lot of stuff that I was interested in. The goal, he said, was to keep the enrollment small—no more than fifty students—so that everybody could have personal attention. Every graduate was expected to go on to a career in the arts.

With the help of the university and with classroom facilities provided by Polytechnic Methodist Church on the university campus, he had created a real conservatory right in my own backyard.

The program seemed perfect for me. But the problem was that the tuition was going to be thirty-five hundred dollars a year, and there was no way that Gertrude or I could have come up with that kind of extra money. When we realized we wouldn't be able to pay for it, I gave up the dream and went back to Wyatt for the eleventh grade.

But one day, just a few weeks after the semester started, the headmaster of the arts school called our house and asked if I could come back by his office. It turned out that some unknown donor had made a bequest to the conservatory to help deserving young people who couldn't afford the tuition. Dr. Schooler said that if I was still interested, there was a place at the conservatory with my name on it.

I can't even begin to tell you what kind of rainbow that was for me at that moment. Not just because of the musical education I would be receiving at the school but because it was a chance to get away from an environment that was killing me. PYC came at just the right moment, and it was like a drink of cold water to my thirsty soul.

Suddenly I had something to commit myself to—a place to go where they understood creative people. There is no question that the scholarship changed things for me—overnight!

If I had stayed at Wyatt High School where the pressures were so intense, I'm not sure I would have made it. I would probably have gone back to drinking and smoking pot and other things that would have held me back and kept me from ever discovering my potential. So, for the chance to break out of that and to get a good, practical education at a school dedicated to the performing arts, I will be eternally grateful.

My academics were bad; the teachers at PYC could see that from my transcript. But they were willing to help me. The lucky thing was that there were only about thirty students in the whole school at that point, so they had time to work with me individually. Everybody there was an artist or a performer of some kind.

Kirk Franklin

All the way through school, right up to that moment in the fall of 1987, I had felt weird, strange, and like a misfit. But as soon as I arrived at PYC, I found out that everybody there was just like me! None of them had fit in either, and none of them were comfortable in a traditional academic setting. They were all artists, musicians, actors, and dancers. What an incredible relief to find out that, here at least, I could fit in and be considered normal!

I'll never forget my last day at O. D. Wyatt. The kids in my class were blown away when they heard that I was going to a music conservatory on a university campus. One guy said, "What are you saying? You mean, out of all the kids in Fort Worth, you've been selected to go to a school for the performing arts?" I nodded and smiled, and he grabbed my hand and said, "Yo, baby, I ain't mad at'cha!" He was excited for me, and so was I.

They didn't know anything about the school, of course. It had only been open a couple of years, and it was small. But it sounded impressive, and I think they thought I must be somebody special after all. I really got a kick out of that for as long as it lasted.

Mrs. Kelly had arranged a little going-away party for me, and a few of the other kids came by to say good-bye. They wished me good luck and patted me on the back, but they had no idea how important this new opportunity was for me. My teachers and friends had seen that I was unhappy, but I don't think any of them knew just how stressed I really was or what a great relief the new school was going to be.

Church Boy

A PLACE APART

PYC was a place for me to get away. It was a place where I could stretch a little bit and find out who I was. I mean, these were the days when my hair was all different colors, and I was really pushing the limits. As it turned out, I was the only black guy chosen to go there. Of the thirty students in the school, there were three or four Hispanics, two black girls, and me, and the rest were white. We made an interesting mix.

I developed a good friendship with two of the guys, Perry and Jason. They were my boys. Perry was a singer, and Jason was an actor. Unlike me, they both came from families who had money. Obviously, anyone who could afford the tuition for a school like that would have to have a little extra cash. But money or class was not really an issue. We were all artists.

I was seventeen, and hanging out with these kids was a trip. I even dated one of the girls. It was the first time I'd ever gone out with somebody who wasn't black. By this time I had a certain spirituality about me and was trying to live a Christian life, but I was still young and immature in my ability to express it.

Every now and then I would spend time with my son's mother. Even though neither of us was very happy and the relationship was extremely difficult—we were like oil and water and didn't mix well at all. I feel the main reason we continued to have any contact is because we knew and hung out with some of the same people.

PYC was small and had very few facilities of its own, but having a college campus surrounding it, there were lots of other resources that helped support the school. There was a Methodist church at the southeast corner of the Texas Wesleyan University campus. That church let us use the piano in the sanctuary for practice and rehearsals during the day. For me, that was one of the best parts.

To be in that big sanctuary by myself, playing the big Steinway piano, was a truly wonderful experience. Except for the colored light that filtered in through the stained glass windows, it was dark in there, giving the place a very special feeling. It was peaceful, and there was a sense of holiness to it, just as there should have been.

One of my teachers, Mrs. Como, was especially helpful to me, and she taught me a lot. She told me to stop trying to be somebody else and to start being myself. She showed me how my own background and experiences could help shape my life as a musician. She told me that the best music comes from the heart and that I needed to relax and let that energy well up from my soul. The fact that she was a black woman and had already been down the road I was traveling gave her words credibility.

She was the only one at the school who really understood my culture. She had been a recording artist with a gospel group in Detroit, and she knew what my music was all about. She was cool, and it was great to have a teacher who had been there and made records.

This school did recruiting tours around the state, and

the year I went on the tour we traveled on a chartered bus to small towns all over West Texas. That was cool, except that most of the time we were in redneck towns and country places that had never really seen a young black man up close.

We didn't stay in hotels, but they had arranged for us to stay with families in a lot of these out-of-the-way places. So you can imagine what some of those families must have thought when they found out that a little black boy was going to spend the night in their front bedroom! But I must say, everybody was nice to me, and I really enjoyed myself.

The tour was great. One night Perry and I stepped outside. We were talking and found out that we were both believers. After that we became very close and would encourage each other about spiritual things.

Jason was my buddy because we were into a lot of the same stuff. He was into clothes; he had a Jeep. He was a white kid, but he acted black. He had some skills. He was cocky, and he had attitude. Besides, he liked black girls. It would have been nothing for him to date a black girl. He would have done it just to be with me. I haven't seen either one of those guys in years, but I remember the good times we had back then. We really used to kick it!

That was my first introduction to white culture, and it was basically a good experience. I was dating a white girl who went there, but we had to keep it quiet. She didn't want her mom to know, and we didn't really want the other kids to know either.

Hanging around with Perry, going over to his house and seeing how his family lived, what they ate, and hearing the types of conversation they had was a learning experience. It was really interesting to see the differences between their lives and my own.

Unfortunately, the school didn't have a lot of juice, and they finally had to shut it down—mainly, I think, because it was more expensive to run than anyone had expected. But I'm convinced it was all part of the plan. It opened a year or two before I came and closed down a year or two after I left.

Whatever else happened at PYC during those years, it remains as one of the most important steppingstones in my maturing as a person and a musician. It gave me a foundation that changed my life, and I'll always be grateful for that.

During that year, the Humble Hearts went through several changes, and eventually we started breaking up. It was probably because I was changing—not so much spiritually but from a creative standpoint. I was becoming a different person. I was beginning to write my own music. I was performing all the time and thinking about forming another group. So the chemistry of that original group began to break down, and I suspect that was for the best.

I don't want to give the impression that everything was great at the new school. There was one teacher in particular who never understood me, and we never did get along. I realize now that I wasn't the only one dealing with new relationships and new cultures. Some of the teachers and some of the other students were seeing black culture for the first time. We were all learning new stuff and not always dealing with it very well.

At the same time, some of the little white girls started liking me, and I started liking them. There were times when it felt like *Guess Who's Coming to Dinner*, and I was Sidney Poitier!

A SPECIAL CALLING

The custodian of the Methodist church where I practiced was an old black pastor who became a good friend to me during those years. He was so deep and spiritual it was awesome just to be around him.

Sometimes when I'd skip an academic class, I'd go down to the basement of the church and talk to him. He took a special interest in me and encouraged me to put my trust in God and to allow Him to focus my abilities and interests. During that first year he became someone I really looked up to. He was powerful.

This church was an intimate place for me; in some ways being there was like being on the roof had been for me when I was a kid. It was a place where I could get away and work out my emotions and my fears. I could get into my zone. I didn't realize it then, but I was creating intimacy with God. As I got older I learned how this comes about, but it was a new experience for me in those days. During that time I was evolving, spiritually and musically, and the church was a great place to be alone with Him.

I was in the church one day, playing for myself, and I had been feeling certain things spiritually when, all of a sudden, a guy ran into the sanctuary from outside. He was a Mexican American wearing earphones, and his eyes were wild and crazy looking. I didn't know what was going on. Who was this guy? It really scared me at first.

He came up to where I was sitting and said, "Man, I was just walking by outside the church, and I heard this music and had to come inside!" And he just kept going on like that, telling me stuff, and I was getting more and more nervous. I kept looking around for the janitor or for a security guard or somebody else to help me in case this guy was totally deranged. But he said, "Please! Please don't stop playing."

So, naturally, I did as he said; I started playing again. As I played through several songs and hymns—whatever came into my mind—I looked over and saw this guy just fall on his face beside the altar and start worshiping God. After several minutes, when I came to a stopping place, I went over to the altar and sat down beside him. I was just seventeen, but my spiritual man was growing. I felt a sense of God's presence.

As soon as I sat down, the guy reached out, took my hand, and started kissing it. He said, "Man, I don't know who you are, but you just saved my life. Thank you, thank you, thank you!"

Church Boy

I was totally perplexed, sitting there wide-eyed and trying to figure out what in the world was going on. But the guy got up as suddenly as he had come in and ran out the back door of the church.

Ever since I had been traveling with the Humble Hearts and going into a lot of different churches, I had begun to see a bigger picture of how different people worship God. Up until we started that group, I had only been at Mount Rose Baptist, and that was my whole frame of reference. But now I was more receptive to other experiences and to other ways of worshiping.

When the guy ran out of the church, I followed him to the back door and looked out to see what he was doing. He had his hands up in the air, worshiping and praying all the way down the street.

As strange as it was, that experience impacted my heart so much that I had to go downstairs to the basement, to the janitor's office, to see what he would make of what had just happened. I told this old pastor everything, from the beginning, and said I wanted to get his reaction.

He thought about it for a minute or two then said, "The only thing I can say, Kirk, is turn around." I turned around in my chair and looked on the back wall, and there was that famous picture of Jesus standing at the door and knocking. "I'm saying, just go to God," he told me. "Tell Him you hear Him, and whatever He's saying, the answer is yes."

Any other time those words might have come as a surprise to me, but I was ready for them at that moment. I was hungry for a deeper experience of God, and I knew I wanted more. So I went back upstairs to the chapel, got down on my knees and prayed sincerely, "Lord, whatever just happened, whatever You're saying to me, I say yes."

When I got back to the school, I went by the room where my friend Perry was working and motioned for him to follow me. We went down the hall to a vacant room, and I said, "I feel God's calling me . . . into ministry."

He was a little surprised, but he was pleased. He was glad to know I felt such a definite calling on my life because he also wanted to know what God was going to do with him.

A few minutes later I got to a phone and called Gertrude at home. I wasn't living with her at that time. She had put me out on Valentine's Day because she got tired of girls calling me all the time! I was living with some friends, but I knew she would want to know about this, so I decided to call.

"Mama," I said, "I'm just calling to tell you that I feel the Lord just called me into the ministry, and I said yes."

All she could say was, "Oh, Kirk! Oh, Kirk!"

She really did love me. She always did, but she didn't always know how to show it.

I think the distance between us occurred because she didn't understand the physical stuff that was going on inside of me. She just couldn't deal with the masculine stuff. Of course, it was never really planned for her to raise me. She was meant to be my covering, and she did that very well.

Church Boy

MANNA FROM HEAVEN

By this time I was at Corinth Church. In my excitement I stopped by the pastor's house and told him about my experience and I felt called to preach. He just said, "Okay."

That's all. No excitement, no congratulations, no sober cautions or fatherly advice. Just, "Okay."

I was playing piano and organ for this church as the minister of music, so the next Sunday morning during his sermon the pastor had me stand up, and he let me have it right in front of the whole congregation. He was from the old school, and although he said he appreciated my musical abilities, he didn't have any patience with any kind of changes, in me or in the church.

He said, "Brothers and sisters, young Mr. Franklin here says he has been called to preach the gospel, and he believes the Lord has given him a calling. Well, Mr. Franklin, we're glad to know it, but there's a few things you've got to do if you think you're going to be a preacher.

"First of all," he said, thumping the pulpit with his open hand, "you're going to have to change the way you dress. Second, you're going to have to change the way you talk. Third, young Mr. Franklin, you're going to have to start being a little more careful about the folks you're seen with."

If I could have melted into the floor, I think I would have disappeared at that moment. But he wasn't finished with me yet. "You've got to clean up your language, your house, your car, everything about you if you want to preach the Word of God. You can't just stand up one Sunday and say you've been anointed to preach, and you can't dress like that if you're going to be a preacher."

Some of the older women were chiming in by this time, echoing back everything he said. But he went on, concluding his little roast by saying, "We're all glad to know you want to use your talents for the kingdom of God, Mr. Franklin, but first you've got to show us that you're a child of the King."

Those words, I'm sorry to say, were not spoken in a spirit of love. I felt that he had dressed me down to make me look small, and I didn't leave the church feeling that I'd been blessed; I felt I'd been cursed. It was as if he were saying that if I wanted to be a preacher, I'd have to go out and get me some preacher suits. Well, the suits I was wearing weren't even my own. I had to borrow them from my roommate, and they were all I had. But this preacher seemed to think that the clothes should come first, before the anointing of God. Maybe that was not his intention but that is how I left feeling.

When I came back that night, the pastor let me deliver a short lay sermon from the front of the church. I was allowed to go up to the pulpit where the pastor was seated, but I couldn't go up on the platform. I had to speak from the area down in front.

He said this was just a way for me to let the others know that I felt God had called me into Christian service; but from that moment on, the word started getting around in the community that Kirk Franklin was going to be a preacher.

By this time I was dating a young woman who was a few years older than I was, and she was about the only one who really celebrated the fact that I was called to preach. She introduced me to her friends as Reverend Franklin, and she encouraged me to study and learn more about my calling.

Even though we didn't stay together very long, it was an important interval for me. After I broke up with her, I continued with the girl I'd been seeing off and on through all those years, and it was that summer—the summer after I'd announced my calling—that I got her pregnant. It wasn't until later in the fall that she knew for sure she was pregnant; but a few weeks after the beginning of my second year at PYC, she came up to the school and told me she was going to have my child.

If I felt I was under pressure before that, suddenly I was in a pressure cooker. My studies slipped, rehearsals slipped, even my work at the church was starting to slip. Then one day early in the second semester of the school year, the teacher who had given me such a hard time ever since I'd arrived at PYC laid into me and said some things she shouldn't have said.

She made me feel really bad. She embarrassed me in front of everybody else, and I couldn't let her get away with that. I probably shouldn't have done it, but I told her what I thought of her words and what she could do with them. If I had been a little more mature in my faith I would have ignored her criticism, but I didn't. Instead I got up, went downstairs, and told the headmaster what had happened.

After we talked about it for a few minutes, Dr. Schooler realized it wasn't going to work out, and he said that maybe this hadn't been such a good idea after all. "I'm sorry you weren't able to make this program work for you, Mr. Franklin," he said. "But I think the best idea may be for you to go ahead and leave school now."

So that's what I did. I walked out the door that afternoon and never went back. That was the end of my high school career.

For a time it felt like the bottom had fallen out of my life. All those people who had doubted my calling, including my pastor at Corinth Church, were seeing all this stuff that was happening to me. I was out of school, I had gotten a girl pregnant, I had been tossed out of Gertrude's house, and now, suddenly, I was on the skids with just about everybody I knew.

It didn't look like there was any way God could ever use a messed-up kid like me. And you can just imagine how I was feeling about all of that.

The amazing thing is that, within two months of that time, I got a call from another church. The pastor wanted to know if I would consider coming over there as minister of music. He told me that the folks at Immanuel Baptist Church needed a music leader and organist, and not only was the money better than I had been making at Corinth but they were going to provide me with a car and employee benefits.

That was just what I needed, and it couldn't have come at a better time. Of course I took the offer. For a seventeen-year-old boy who had just dropped out of high school, it was like manna from heaven.

Where the Spirit of the Lord is
There is liberty.
Where the Spirit of the Lord is
The captives are set free.
The wounded are made whole,
I'll find rest for my soul.

Where the Spirit is
Where the Spirit is
Where the Spirit is
There is liberty.

Where the Spirit of the Lord is
There is liberty.
Where the Spirit of the Lord is
The captives are set free.
The wounded are made whole,
There is rest for my soul.

Where the Spirit is
There is healing.
Where the Spirit is
There is deliverance.
Where the Spirit is
There is joy.

Where the Spirit of the Lord is
There is liberty.

Words and music by Kirk Franklin.
Copyright ©1995, Kerrion Publishing / Lilly Mack Publishing (BMI).
Used by permission.

6

Where the Spirit Is

moved out of Gertrude's house in July 1989, and I was completely on my own for the first time in my life. On Sundays and Wednesdays I had a steady job leading the music at Immanuel Baptist Church, and I was still performing with the Humble Hearts from time to time. But it still wasn't enough to pay my expenses, and I realized I had to find a real job.

There I was, needing a job, tossed out of Gertrude's house, and with a baby on the way. I agreed to help with the expenses for the baby, but marriage was out of the question. We knew that marriage would have been a disaster, just compounding the injury of a relationship that never really was a true commitment and was bad long before there was a baby. In the meantime, I had to find some way of pulling myself together.

By this time, a lot of the kids I had grown up with in Riverside were into drugs, and they were robbing and stealing to pay for their habits. So there could be no more contact there. But to make matters worse, there were also some people I had known through the church who were a bad influence, either because they were living a double life or because they were gay. So no matter which way I turned, I was alone and very much on my own.

The kids I had been hanging out with at the Professional Youth Conservatory had all disappeared from my life by this time. They had been a lot of fun, and we had been friends while I was still at school. But I never saw any of them again after I left.

Finally, in December 1988, I landed a job selling pianos at the mall. It was during the holidays, and the store was pushing pianos and organs for Christmas. So they hired me as a combination demonstrator and salesman. I was supposed to play the pianos and show people how much fun it would be to own one.

That was the easy part. I could get them interested in buying one, but, unfortunately, I was never able to take the next step and make the sale.

I was having so much fun playing the pianos and entertaining people that I wasn't doing much selling. Shoppers walking through the mall would hear the music and come over to where I was jamming, and before long there would be a crowd of forty or fifty people around me. But nobody was buying!

Naturally, I was disappointed. I was getting a small hourly wage; the only way I could make any real money was with the commissions I would earn from making a sale. But I wasn't making any! I was beginning to think I would never be able to hold a regular job like other people. Maybe I wasn't cut out for it. If that were the case, then I needed to find some way of making a living in music.

Just as I was thinking I had nowhere left to turn, a gentleman came over to talk to me. I was sitting there at the piano, probably playing some sort of gospel tune, and he said he liked what I was doing. He introduced himself and told me his name was Roy West and he was the senior minister at Greater Stranger's Rest Baptist Church in West Fort Worth.

Suddenly I remembered that I had met him several months earlier when I had played there with the Humble Hearts. So we got into a conversation, and he asked me what I was doing these days. I said I was trying to make a living selling pianos, but so far the only money I was making was as music minister at Immanuel Baptist Church.

At that point, he asked if I'd be interested in coming over to lead the music at his church. I knew that Stranger's Rest was an outstanding church with a very impressive music program. I didn't have to think very long about my decision.

This seemed like just the opportunity I had been praying for. How could I refuse? I was feeling like a failure at selling pianos, I had all kinds of financial obligations to meet, and I was desperate to start making some money so I could get my life back on track. So I said yes, and that would prove to be a very important step for me.

Stranger's Rest was the church where I was finally able to step out and get my feet wet in the music scene on a bigger scale than I had ever done before. Even though it was located in an area called Como, which was far from where I lived, it was a very popular church and had a well-trained choir that already knew how to sing.

When I left Immanuel, I had to give back the car they had provided for me. I was going to need some wheels of my own, so I went out and bought myself a little Volkswagen bug. It wasn't exactly the image I wanted to project, but at least it was transportation.

I had turned eighteen by the time I started the new job, and I was beginning to get a feel for who I was and what sort of music I wanted to do. It was a good time, and I was beginning to think that maybe there would be an opportunity to take it to another level if I could just keep working at it.

I had been around music all my life, and I had been doing it so long that I couldn't imagine doing anything else. But this was the first time that I thought, *Maybe I can actually make a living at this, and do it, serving God.*

A TURNING POINT

At Stranger's Rest, I had the chance to meet a lot more people in the music scene. The pastor's cousin in Houston had a well-known minister of music named Michael McKay. He was a popular gospel artist, somebody I really admired. As soon as I met him, I knew this was somebody I wanted to be like. That had never happened before.

I had never known even one person of whom I could say, Yeah, that's what I want to be like. But McKay was different. His hobby was body-building. He was muscular and good looking, he knew how to dress, and he had a style all his own. He just had the look. When I saw him I thought, *That's it! I want to be like that.*

Stranger's Rest already had a drummer, and that's the first time that had happened. Most of the churches I had

Kirk Franklin & the Family

God's Property

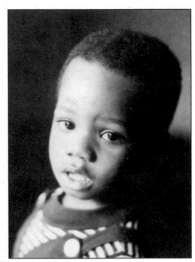

Kirk was adopted at age three by Gertrude Franklin. By age seven, he was offered his first recording contract.

By age fourteen, he was a popular break-dancer.

The house in which Kirk was born and grew up.

Gertrude Franklin in 1943, years before Kirk came into her life.

TCU photo by Jim Winn

The black gospel workshop at Texas Christian University helped give twenty-one-year-old Kirk a little media exposure.

BOTTOM: *Members of the Family gather for a group photo with friends before a 1996 performance.*

Kirk and Tammy at their wedding reception January 20, 1996. Kirk says he married his best friend.

Kirk with his daughter Carrington and son Kerrion.

Photo by Rhea-Engert

TOP: *Kirk and Tammy with Kerrion and Carrington.*

RIGHT: *The Franklin family in front of Buckingham Palace in London, England in July 1996.*

TOP: *Kirk, his wife and children, some of The Family members, and manager Gerald Wright, sightseeing in London.*

BOTTOM: *Kirk runs through a rehearsal and a quick microphone check with members of* God's Property *before their recording session.*

Photo by Rhea-Engert

Kirk and Tammy (at eight months pregnant). Kirk was so excited and proud about his wife's pregnancy that he wanted to take pictures embracing her stomach.

LEFT: *Proud Daddy holding 12-month-old Kennedy Elizabeth. Before he knew Tammy was expecting, Kirk was wishing for a baby girl. Kirk says Kennedy represents a second chance, completeness.*

*The Franklin family posing for one of the pictures used as their 1997
Christmas card. "We refuse to get caught up in yours, mine, and
ours," says Kirk. "God gave us to each other, so we know
our family is God ordained."*

Among the many people instrumental to Kirk's success are Vicki Lataillade (right), President of GospoCentric Records and Monica Bacon (left), Vice-President of GospoCentric Records.

Kirk Franklin, onstage during the 1997 Tour of Life.

During 1996 and 1997, Kirk Franklin and God's Property were invited to perform their hit songs on several televised specials, including Soul Train, Live *from the* Apollo, Late Night with David Letterman, The Tonight Show, *and the highly acclaimed* Savion Glover Special *from New York City.*

Kirk Franklin is one gospel recording artist who has used his influence to spread the good news in virtually every entertainment medium.

Kirk Franklin was co-host of the 1998 Stellar Awards broadcast and recipient of Best Gospel Song and Producer of the Year awards, among many others.

Photo by Rhea-Engert

TOP & BELOW: A 1998 Father's Day photo. "God's gift to me is Tammy and our three children. He has used them to help make who I've become."

Photo by Rhea-Engert

been with didn't have regular bands. I could always bring in drums and supporting instruments when we needed them for programs, musicals, Christmas specials, and things like that. But these guys already had a regular drummer and a bass player too.

But what really made the new position unique was that this was also the first time I didn't have to be at the piano or organ the whole time. I could get up, take the microphone, and lead the music from the platform. That gave me the freedom to direct, to put something together and orchestrate the worship environment, a lot like I do now with the Family. So I started working on how I could make the music a special part of the service.

This was a prominent Baptist church, and in the beginning a lot of people thought I was a little too wild. Maybe I was, at first. But I could see where I wanted it to go. I was still trying to establish who I was—trying to look like, act like, even sing like V. Michael McKay—but I wasn't there yet. So I had to work a little harder to find a style of my own in the right format for these people.

McKay was charismatic, and he was older than I was— around thirty or so at the time. So I looked up to him, and I really looked up to the pastor too. It was obvious that Roy West had a special anointing. And besides that, he was cool. A lot of young people came to this church because of his powerful preaching and his personal style.

On May 7, 1989, my son Kerrion was born. I took his mother to the hospital then went straight back to the church because V. Michael McKay was doing a concert that night. I was so interested in getting into music by this time that even the birth of my son came second to a gospel concert. I think my priorities would be different now, but that's how desperate I was to get something going.

I wanted to do music for a living. I had thought about it a lot, and by this time there was a hunger growing inside me. Nothing fell from heaven and hit me on the head. Nobody walked up and offered me a contract. It just happened. When I went to this church, I developed a hunger to write and minister professionally. Stranger's Rest was a turning point for my musical career.

Before long I was working in two churches at the same time. On Sundays I was music minister at Stranger's Rest, and on Saturdays I was doing the same thing at Grace Temple Seventh Day Adventist Church. I was doing double duty, but I really enjoyed it and needed the work. As it turned out, this second job was how I met the man who would eventually become my business manager, Gerald Wright.

If anything, Adventist churches are even more reserved and traditional than Baptist churches, but I didn't let that stop me! My musical style was a little wild for them at first, but they liked it. The choir started growing, so they didn't complain too loudly. Gerald was the choir director at this church, and he really liked what I was doing, so that helped.

It was no secret that I had fathered a child out of wedlock, so I didn't have to go through all kinds of explanations and excuses. Both these churches were big enough that, even after the baby was born, they could deal with it.

I was eighteen with a child born out of wedlock, and I was working through those issues myself and dealing with the spiritual consequences. But nobody at either Stranger's Rest or Grace Temple threw it in my face. It was as if they were giving me another chance to get myself on track and to be the man I should be—and could be, with God's help.

At the same time, Stranger's Rest was getting better known for our music, and new people were coming to the church because they had heard what was happening there. We were developing a really good sound, and one day I mentioned to Pastor West that I'd like to produce an album of our music. He said he thought that was a good idea, and he advanced me enough money on my paycheck to put something together.

The first thing I did was call V. Michael McKay and another guy who understood the production side. I asked if they'd like to come up and help me. They said yes, so we produced my first recording in the sanctuary at Stranger's Rest. That was in 1989, and in those days the "in" thing was to do recordings of gospel music with a live audience. So that's what we did.

I tried to do the album on my own. I didn't really have the skills for it since it was my first effort at something like that. V. Michael McKay helped me with the recording as much as he could, but I don't think it was meant for him to be very involved. I just did the best I could with my limited knowledge. We made the recording, and I thought we did a good job.

I had used all of my own songs on the recording, including "Psalm 51," "Every Day with Jesus," and one or two others that I had written over the last couple of years. But it didn't go any further than that. I wanted something on tape to show what we could do, and I hoped that maybe something would come of it. But I didn't know how to take the next step, finding a record producer. So, for the time being, all I had to show for my work was that tape.

WALKING THE WALK

God was allowing me to develop a little bit of a name for myself, getting a little popularity and getting a little juice rolling. I was still struggling with income, because any fame I'd had up to that point was purely by association. To help conserve my resources, I moved in with Gerald Wright and started looking for a day job.

I looked a long time but never found anything that suited my skills, so I finally took a job, through a temporary service, unloading trucks.

I wasn't especially strong or physical. I had never been much of an athlete, and I certainly wasn't very big. By the end of the first day I thought I was going to die. By the end of the second day, I wished I could. I managed to stay on the job exactly one week until I collapsed, totally exhausted. I decided that was no kind of work for a piano player!

Fortunately, a few music jobs started coming my way

after that, and before long I got a call from my old teacher from O. D. Wyatt High School, Jewell Kelly, asking if I'd like to do some work with the Dallas/Fort Worth Mass Choir. She was director of the Fort Worth Mass Choir and was very involved in the whole gospel music scene at that time. The choir was put together by Milton Biggham.

Once again, it was an easy decision. I said I'd love to do it, and a couple of weeks later we started into preparations. On the last night of the conference, in June 1990, we did a recording that included my song "Every Day with Jesus."

Up to that point, Dallas had always been the big show for gospel workshops; Fort Worth was somewhere down in the fine print. I wasn't getting any attention at home. But once I started going over to work with the D/FW Mass Choir, I started getting to know some of the movers and shakers in the gospel community, and my name was getting around.

I thought maybe the tape I had recorded at Stranger's Rest could be a door opener for me. Even though I felt the recording was a failure at the time and even though I was disappointed that nothing ever came of it, I thought it still might be of some use in showing people what I could do. So I made sure I always had a copy with me.

Jewell Kelly was the director of the Fort Worth choir, and the director of the Dallas choir was a guy named Bubba. Jewell was a good friend, and she wanted to give me a shot with some of my songs. But she felt she had to give all the other songwriters equal time. So I didn't get as much opportunity to perform my stuff as I would have liked when Jewell was directing. But it was good exposure. I was becoming better known, and I think they realized that the songs that God gave me were pretty good.

Unfortunately, the guy in Dallas was unscrupulous, and he didn't bother about little things like copyrights or even saying thank you when he used somebody else's material. He took my song "Joy" and included it on a mass-choir album that he recorded in North Carolina later that year. He even listed himself as the author on the album cover.

He didn't give me any recognition or any money, and my name was never mentioned anywhere on the album. I'm not sure what I would have done if he had made any money out of it. Fortunately, the album didn't sell enough copies to worry about, and that was pretty much the end of it.

From that point on, it seemed like steppingstones had been laid in my path. It wasn't quite as clear to me when I was going through it, but looking back on it now I can see how God had orchestrated every step of the way. First, I was invited to participate in gospel workshops and mass-choir events in Fort Worth. That led, in turn, to an invitation to lead the D/FW Mass Choir, and that was a big break for me.

For a Fort Worth boy to be invited to lead the D/FW Mass Choir was very special. I was a little nervous at first, but it was a great opportunity. I really enjoyed it. The best part was that I would have a chance to meet Milton Biggham, who was the big deal in gospel music. He had been invited to Dallas to hold a series of workshops and to oversee the taping of the "conference album" we would be recording live during the concert on the last night of the rehearsal.

As I was getting ready to go over to Dallas, I realized that if I could just get Milton Biggham to take a look at my work, maybe he could give my ministry a boost. I didn't have very much to show, but just in case I could get a minute with him, I stuck my extra copy of the Stranger's Rest tape in my bag. I could at least do that. And sure enough, one afternoon I spotted Mr. Biggham coming down the hall.

As soon as I saw him coming, I went over and said, "Mr. Biggham, I'm Kirk Franklin. I'm the minister of music at Stranger's Rest Church in Fort Worth, and I wonder if you'd be willing to listen to a tape of some songs we recorded."

He told me he was in a hurry at the moment, but he took the tape and said he'd listen to it whenever he had an extra minute. Knowing how busy he was and knowing that most people don't really keep their promises, I doubted that he would actually do it. But when I saw him the next morning he called out to me from across the room.

He motioned for me to come over, and as I got closer, he said, "Boy, I listened to your tape. You're pretty good. And you play the piano, don't you?"

I said, "Yes sir, I sure do."

He said my songs were good, but he really liked my piano playing. He was going to need somebody to play for him, and he wanted to know if I had a number I could do with the whole choir.

"Yes sir!" I said. "Did you listen to the song 'Every Day with Jesus' on my tape?"

"Yeah," he said. "That's a good song. I like it just fine. Can you do that with the mass choir?"

"Sure," I said without hesitation. "I sure can, Mr. Biggham."

"All right, then. I want you to do it in rehearsal, and if it sounds good we'll do it on the tape Friday night."

I couldn't believe my ears. They were going to record my song on the conference album for the D/FW Mass Choir! But he didn't stop there. Milton also said he could see that I was a good music leader and he would like for me to help out by directing the choir and leading some of the rehearsals during the week.

My heart was racing. I was thrilled. Not only would I be doing something I loved but Milton Biggham was "the man" in gospel music, and I knew that the recognition I would get by hanging around with him could only help.

After that, I was a little better known. But when I got back home to Fort Worth, I was feeling let down. I had had a chance to meet some important people and lead the mass choir, and I even had one of my songs recorded. But I was convinced that was about as far as it would go. I assumed everything would just settle back into a normal routine, and I would just pick up my duties at the church as if nothing had happened.

Church Boy

Even though I didn't have a lot to show for my efforts, I now believe that was the time my professional career really began. I was becoming better known all over the metroplex as a pianist, and before long I was getting invitations to take part in gospel workshops in Fort Worth, Dallas, and other places all over the country. I started to think that this stuff might actually go somewhere after all.

INDECENT EXPOSURE

The most important gospel music organization in the country is the Gospel Music Workshop of America, or GMWA. The association was started by the late Rev. James Cleveland, one of the first gospel artists to have a hit song make the national pop charts. Over the years the GMWA has become an important voice for African Americans and a major institution in the gospel music community.

The GMWA holds a national convention each year in different cities around the country. And the person who guided the GMWA Choir throughout the eighties and early nineties was Milton Biggham.

One day Milton called and said he wanted me to direct "Every Day with Jesus" at the mass choir in Washington, D.C. So in August 1990 I got on a plane and flew to the nation's capital.

I couldn't believe it. There I was, a twenty-year-old kid from Fort Worth, Texas, flying off to Washington, D.C, and mixing with all those bigwigs. I got there on Monday morning, and they had me on the program the first day.

They set us up for Monday, Tuesday, and Wednesday rehearsals plus a Thursday review and a final run-through.

On Friday we would be giving a concert for an audience of more than twenty thousand people, and that's when we would make the live recording for that event. That's how they're able to do an entire album in one week.

I was still an outsider—just a wannabe—but all of a sudden I was hanging out with Milton Biggham, and that gave me some name recognition. He gave me the juice.

Milton had introduced me, and since he was the main man, I was invited to what most people considered to be the single most important gospel workshop in the country. I was participating in week-long workshops, helping to rehearse the choir each day, then taking part in the live recording on Friday night. I had seen it done many times, but this time I was right in the big middle of it all.

What an incredible experience it turned out to be! I can't even put into words all the feelings and emotions I was going through as I flew to Washington, D.C., and saw the nation's capital for the first time. I took a taxi from National Airport to the theater downtown where we would be working and was thrilled to finally meet all the incredibly talented musicians and singers who had come in from all over the country.

It was awesome! Not only were we going to record my song on a major label but they were paying me fifteen hundred dollars just to be there. For a young man in my situation, that was serious money.

Church Boy

To cap it off, I knew that Milton Biggham liked my stuff and wanted to use me as one of his music leaders. At one point, he put his arm around my shoulder and said, "You're a good man, Kirk Franklin. You're a good musician, and I could use somebody like you."

He didn't offer me a lot of money or a big recording contract or anything like that, but he said he would let me hang around with him and sort of be his "boy." In that venue, that was like a stamp of approval from one of the most important men in the business. I knew this could be a big break for me.

I said, "I'll stick to you like glue, Mr. Biggham, if that's what you want."

All that week, the word got around that Kirk Franklin was Milton Biggham's boy. Everywhere he went, I was there. When he needed somebody on the piano, I played. When he said frog, I jumped! Consequently, my stock started going up, and the girls started hanging around with me. They all thought I was the new "Big Willie"!

First thing Monday morning, Milton said, "Kirk, I want you to rehearse the choir and teach them your song. Will you do that?" The only song of mine he really knew was "Every Day with Jesus," which we had performed in Dallas. But he liked it, and for him, that was my trademark song.

Altogether, there were three thousand singers, songwriters, pianists, and directors from all over the world in the performance hall that day. By the time they were assembled and ready, I was pretty nervous. I wasn't at

Mount Rose Baptist anymore. This was the National Mass Choir in Washington, D.C., and I was supposed to go out there in front of all those people and teach them my song!

I thought I was going to choke, and that's just what I did.

When I got out on stage in front of all those wonderful, highly experienced veteran musicians and singers, I was weak in the knees. I started by telling them a little bit about the song and how I would like to go through it. Then I played it through one time on the piano.

But as soon as I stood up to start teaching it, I completely lost it. I mean, I was stuttering and bumbling and making a fool of myself, and everybody standing up there on the risers must have thought I was a total idiot. Nothing worked, and the sound was all wrong.

Finally, I just stopped, put down the music and said, "People, I'm sorry. I'm new at this, and I've got to tell you, I'm so nervous being out here in front of so many great musicians, I'm just making a fool of myself. I want you to know how embarrassed I am. Will you please forgive me?"

All of a sudden, it was like they had fallen in love with me. They could see that I was young, and I guess they felt sorry for me. Or maybe they just appreciated my honesty. But they started laughing and smiling and encouraging me.

One man up in the middle of the choir said, "Hey, Kirk, don't you worry about it, son. Let's just sing the song. You're going to do just fine."

Well, I took a deep breath and went back to the music, and sure enough, it went very well after that. In fact, it went great. By the time we finished rehearsing, everybody thought I was great. They were patting me on the back and thanking me for being there, and they made me feel like a hero for a little while.

Man, I was the Howard Hughes of gospel music that day! The rest of the day the word got out: "That's the kid who taught everybody his song, and he's bad!" Of course that meant, *He's good!*

I couldn't believe it. Everywhere I went after that, people would speak to me and smile, and I could hear them talking about "that nice young man who led the choir." By this time, the girls really thought I was hot, and they wanted to hang with me.

I was enjoying all that, and it was really a great week. Then Friday night came, and it was my turn to lead the choir again. We were going to record "Every Day with Jesus," so I went back onstage with my music and got everything ready.

But what happened with me blowing up that big was that I got the big head. I had been walking around signing autographs and hanging out, and I didn't go back and review my song until Thursday night. Man, I got up at the rehearsal and absolutely flopped. I wasn't really worried about it, though, because we had done it so well on Monday. I figured we could do it again. But on Friday night at the actual recording session we did the number, and it was horrible!

The song didn't work, and it died a slow, horrible, painful death. It was obvious to everybody, not just me, that something wasn't right. I couldn't keep the singers together, and they kept missing entrances. Besides that, the band was doing stuff I had never even heard before, and it was turning out all wrong.

Suddenly everybody realized the kid had blown it, and the proof was right there in living stereo for the whole world to hear! I couldn't get out of there fast enough. I said good-bye and thank you. Then I walked back to my hotel and just lay down in the bed and sobbed.

A FUTURE AND A HOPE

Fortunately, when I got back home to Fort Worth nobody knew anything about my big blowup. They only knew that I had been up to direct the National Mass Choir in Washington, D.C., and everybody thought that was really cool.

It didn't take long for me to realize that things were going to be different from now on. People knew me as the guy who had played for Milton Biggham. I had also played for V. Michael McKay when he did his workshop in Dallas. So whenever the big names came to town to do a workshop, I was one of the ones they called.

All the big national gospel artists were coming through Dallas/Fort Worth, too, and I was one who would come over to play for them. Before long I was teaching all the songs I had been writing since 1987 to community choirs and gospel workshops in Texas and many other places all over the country. I was going from coast to coast and loving every minute of it.

The girls back home were starting to warm up to me too. They were all into the gospel music scene, and since I had made such a miserable flop on the D.C. recording, I thought it was going to go back to the usual. But they didn't know anything about that. They just knew I'd been up to GMWA, and my star was shining as bright as ever.

I still didn't have my life together, though. By the time I got back from D.C., I had already moved out of Gerald's house. I was only there a short time, but I'd worn out my welcome. So I moved in with another friend. Between July 1989 and November 1990, I moved at least twelve times, and I didn't have anything close to a regular life during all that time.

On the music side, however, things were warming up. Other than V. Michael McKay and Yolanda Adams, plus a few more, I was one of the only ones from Texas who had been involved in the GMWA recordings. Chicago, Detroit, Los Angeles, and Atlanta were the big venues for gospel music; but here I was in Fort Worth with at least a foot in the door and traveling most of the time. Thanks to my friendship with Milton Biggham, I was starting to make some moves.

In the process, I was also able to move from being a piano player to being a director. I was getting a bit of a reputation for that. One reason people would ask me to direct is that I was a clown. In a lot of choirs, the director is more or less invisible, but in gospel music, the director is part of the show. He does stuff and moves around a lot. So I would get up and entertain the people, and they enjoyed it.

I remember a couple of times I even directed with my feet! I would stomp or jump up on a certain downbeat. Sometimes I would kick my foot in the air, and the drums would make a loud pop and stuff like that. People who had been brought up on straight gospel music got a kick out of my antics on stage—no pun intended!

But there I was, in the odd situation of getting a little bit of exposure and popularity and a little bit of a reputation while my life was still a mess. I didn't have a place to live, and I was still wrestling with all kinds of insecurities and the flesh. But because I was known as Milton's boy, people were treating me with respect.

Over the next several months, Milton Biggham gave me the chance to travel with him, and that took care of my living arrangements as long as I was on the road. During the week I was Milton's piano player, and on weekends I would be back home directing two choirs and leading the music at two different churches.

With GMWA workshops going on all the time in cities all over the country, I was starting to get a lot of calls to lead workshops on my own, and before long I realized that I needed to start praying about starting my own group. I had been keeping track of some of the singers I had known over the years, so I started calling a few of them to see whether or not they might be interested in doing something with me.

Church Boy

One of the first people I called was a young woman I had known at Mount Rose Baptist when I was just eleven years old. She was interested, and she's still with me today as a singer with the Family. Eventually I had a core group of fifteen regulars on board.

Along the way one of my songs was used without authorization by a guy named Bubba who put it on an album with a North Carolina choir. I eventually recorded it with the Georgia Mass Choir. Oddly enough, a few years later I got a call from a Hollywood producer who said he'd heard my song "Every Day with Jesus" on an album I did with Georgia Mass, and he liked what he heard.

Years after Bubba took my song and used it on his North Carolina album, these people heard it, liked it, and selected it for the soundtrack of their movie *The Preacher's Wife*, starring Denzel Washington and Whitney Houston. Fortunately, this time my name was on it.

Melodies from heaven
Rain down on me, rain down on me;
Take me in Your arms and hold me close
Rain down on me, rain down on me;
Fill me with your precious Holy Ghost
Rain down on me, rain down on me.

7

Melodies from Heaven

It was a Wednesday night in November of 1990. I was not living at home, but would call to check on Gertrude regularly. This particular night she did not answer, which seemed strange, because it was late and she was eighty years old. I felt something was wrong, so I called my best friend Jon Drummond to go with me to check on my mother. When we got there, the lights were off and the dog she always kept in the house was outside. My continued knocking and screaming that received no answer made me panic, and soon I woke up the neighbors. The neighbors called the fire department. When they arrived, I'll never forget their words as they flashed their flashlights through her window. "There is someone in the bed asleep." I don't remember how I felt then or what I was thinking. All I knew is that night I lost my Mama!

Gertrude's death was hard for me. That old woman had taken me in and loved me when my own mother walked away. She held me close and told me I was somebody. She made sure I understood that Jesus loved me and that everything else was going to be okay.

She fed me, clothed me, took me wherever I needed to go in her old car, and never resented doing whatever she had to do to help me have a better life, no matter how trivial or demeaning it might be—even picking up aluminum cans along the roadside so she could afford to pay Mrs. Jackson for my music lessons.

When Gertrude passed away, part of me rejoiced for her because I knew with all my heart that she was going to a better place. But for the other part of me, the human part, that was one of the most heart-breaking moments of my life.

Sitting alone in my room one night months later, after coming home from a very successful performance, I found myself drawn into a quiet, gentle reverie. Before I knew it, I was literally overcome by a wave of nostalgia about those early years, growing up in our rough Riverside neighborhood in West Fort Worth.

I realized that it was Gertrude who should get most of the credit for all the good things that were beginning to happen for me. After all, she had been the one who had worked so hard to get me where I was. She had always been there, waiting up for me, praying for me, jacking me up when I needed it, but always trying to keep my eyes focused on Jesus.

As I looked around the room that night, I saw musical programs and tapes and CDs of all kinds, each one reminding me of the things I had done and the places I'd been as a musician. I was on the verge of becoming a national recording artist and a successful performer. There was a new momentum in my life and career at that time. But what stood out in my memory was not my achievements and not the discord or the disappointments of the last few years. It was all the good times and all the happy memories of my youth.

I remembered driving home from church one night in Gertrude's old car when I was no more than seven or eight years old. We had been to a musical program at Corinth Church, and I was really excited about it.

Corinth Church was a well-known gospel church; it put on musicals that were monsters. When they put on their annual choir concerts, practically every gospel fan in Fort Worth showed up. It was just a tiny church, but when that place started rocking, there was rejoicing in heaven!

The guy who put it all together was an incredible musician named Sammy Samington, and he was one big boy, weighing in at four hundred pounds or better. He was over all the choirs, and he had a very contemporary style.

I never realized I had a heart for gospel music before that night, but all the way home from church I couldn't stop talking. I was blown away by what we had just heard, and I knew then that, somehow or other, I was going to be involved in gospel music. I had been interested in it before that in a small way but mainly because it was part of my culture and heritage. I liked the sound. But that night I realized that I had a serious interest in doing gospel music.

What made it so special was that everybody at Corinth

Church was a singer. The congregation was known for that; literally everybody at that church had pipes.

Gertrude talked to Sammy about my playing, and on one occasion, he let me play a song at one of the youth musicals. His concept was to make every number a big production number; for that number he had me on the piano, another little boy on the organ, and a friend of mine on the drums. So it was like a little jamfest.

The major musicals were put on by the adult choir, and they were just awesome. Many years before, after coming home from one of those musicals, I slipped into bed and lay there with the window open, just thinking about all we'd seen. We didn't have air conditioning in those days, so I just lay there with the breeze blowing through the window and started humming the melody to Elton John's song, "Benny and the Jets."

The song was being played on all the radio stations at that time. I could hear the melody in my head, but I had my own words. I started singing to myself, "He's coming back. He's coming back. I know the Bible says He's coming back!" And little by little, I put the whole song together in my mind. That was the first time I can actually remember doing anything like that.

There were lots of things that brought melodies and words to my mind when I was a little kid. I remembered those times, so long ago. Once again I was that little kid sitting up on the roof late at night, staring up at the stars, humming songs and singing to myself. I was trying to figure out what it all meant, what was going on with my life.

Sometimes I would be sitting up there, crying, singing, touching heaven, and hoping it would all come out right in the end.

Why did I do that? I don't know. Maybe I thought I could make sense of it all if I sat up there long enough. Maybe I was trying to reach up and grab a little piece of eternity with my thoughts and my prayers. There would be many times over the next few years when I would let life get the best of me—times when I couldn't keep up with all my responsibilities. Most things in my life came so fast and so unexpectedly I made a mess of a lot of them.

But there was one important fact I couldn't escape. It was impossible. It couldn't happen in the real world. But somehow or other, Gertrude Franklin had made her little lost boy into a gospel singer.

ONCE FROM THE TOP

By the time I turned twenty-two years old in 1992 I had written several songs for other choirs to record, but I really wanted to come up with my own thing. I felt compelled to try something, so I decided to get together with several friends I'd known for a long time.

I called Tam, David, Mousey, Dalon, Theresa, Keisha, Chris, Darryl, Byron, Mona, Cassie, Yolanda, Dee, Stephanie, Jeanette, Sheila, and Jon Drummond, and we all got together for a trial run. I wanted to know if they thought we should try to do something together; I wanted to see if we could start some kind of group. They thought it was a good idea, and all of them said they wanted to give it a try.

Our first rehearsal was in April 1992 in the recreation room at the apartments where I lived, and we caused quite a commotion. Neighbors were coming outside to listen. Others were hanging out the windows, saying, "Hey, what is all that singing?" Before we finished that first meeting, we knew that God was doing something. We could see that our audience was enjoying what it heard, and that was a sign of encouragement.

Over the years there have been a lot of other singers who have played an important part in the group. Some had other jobs or interests that took them away. Some have gone on to musical careers of their own apart from this group. In some cases they've had a different idea about where we were going or what our sound should be like.

But the group we have today grew out of that first meeting, and when I named the group the "Family," it was because those people truly are my family. I dearly love them. In a sense, they're all the family I've ever known.

David Mann has always been like a brother to me; we go back to my early teenage years. In the Family we call him Big Daddy, and he was one of the first people I called back in 1992. He was with me in Memphis when I fell. His wife, Tam, is one truly anointed sister. I really believe the Spirit is on her when she sings.

Church Boy

I met Dalon Collins in 1990 when I was working with the D/FW Mass Choir. He really blew me away because he was so gifted and so humble. He's just a big teddy bear with a heart for God. I would put Dalon up against any other gospel singer. Somebody nicknamed him Big Love, and that's a good choice. He's just incredible. Dalon is going to have an album of his own very soon, and when that happens, hold on to your hat. You're going to hear some music!

Keisha Gandy is like my little sister. She has been through a lot, and she, more than anybody else in the Family, reminds me of myself. She wasn't raised by her parents, and she went through a lot of trauma growing up. She has such a giving heart. She's going to make somebody a great wife, and she's got a real future as a singer. She's not a straight gospel singer; in fact, I think she may wind up singing more traditional music or jazz, but she's got real talent.

Sheila Brice has the nickname of "Mother" in the Family. In some ways, she's like the great old gospel singer, Mother Smith. She's the one who keeps us all together.

Carrie Young Collins, better known as "Mousey," has a wonderful voice. She knows who she is, and she loves God with all her heart. She's raising three kids on her own and sacrifices to travel with us. That's how committed she is.

Another singer is a young lady named Demetrice "Dee" Clinkscale. She brings so much energy. She's not with us on every road trip, but if I could I'd take her everywhere I go.

Theresa Rucker and Jeanette Johnson are two singers I can always depend on. They always have my back, always reliable.

I sometimes tease Terri Pace, saying that she's the spoiled baby of this gang. She's terrific, and she's a young lady who knows what she wants!

John Grey was one of the last guys in the group and has given us some diversity, since he's always a comedian. He's like having a younger brother.

Jon Drummond is as talented in track and field as he is in music—he's an Olympic sprinter. At one time he was my roommate, and he's one of the best friends a guy could ever have.

Darrell Blair is as solid as a rock, and he has a tremendous solo voice. He is now pursuing his own ministry full time.

Yolanda McDonald is Miss Sensitive. She's got sensitivity coming out of her ears.

Stephanie Glynn is a true lady. We call her "Chicken," but she walks and talks like a lady.

We knew from the first night that we had a sound of our own and that it would be good if we could do something with it. So I started working on a lot of original music, and after we had done several successful concert dates, playing and singing in churches in the area, I thought it would be a good idea to see if we couldn't produce an album of our best songs.

Church Boy

A deacon at the church approached me about doing a project because he believed in what we were doing. That was our first big step.

After a lot of planning and organizing, we made a live recording that would become our demo tape. We put together some promotional materials about the group and our experience then sent off several copies to some of the major record labels. By December 1992, we had two or three solid offers and several expressions of interest.

One of the companies really liked our sound and sent one of its vice presidents to sit down with us and talk about a contract. But during the negotiations process, I got a note that another company in Los Angeles, a new label called GospoCentric Records, had heard about us and was interested in our project.

I had previously given a tape to a gospel artist by the name of Daryl Coley. In a few days we got a call back from the president of the company, Vicki Lataillade. She said she loved our music and wanted to make an offer. I don't know why I agreed. GospoCentric was a tiny, new company with almost no track record, and the others we were talking to were huge by comparison. But I felt led to sit down with this lady and hear what she had to say. She was a spiritual sister, and I sensed that she knew just what we were talking about.

Unlike those big labels and their impressive sales pitches, Vicki didn't spend all her time boasting about how great her company was or how much money it could make for us the first six months. Instead, she talked about her passion to serve God, to spread the Word, and to change people's lives through the medium of gospel music.

Then she said something I'll never forget.

"Kirk," she said, "I know you can find a lot of other labels out there with more money and more power than we've got, but you'll never find one that will work harder for you. We think your music is great, and you would be a very important artist for us, not just one of a hundred newcomers on the list."

Vicki had started GospoCentric from scratch. She started the company with a six-thousand-dollar loan from her father's civil service pension, trusting that God would bring talented artists to her if she dedicated everything to Him. That really hit me hard, because I'd done almost the same thing with the five thousand dollars I had borrowed to cut the demo Vicki wanted to produce.

"If this is what God wants, Kirk," she said, "He will confirm it in you. So I'm not asking you to sign a contract right now. All I'm asking you to do is to pray about it and see what God wants you to do. I'll do the same thing, and then we'll get back together and find out what you've decided."

So that's what we did. I prayed, she prayed, everybody in the Family prayed, and three days later I called her back and said, "Vicki, if you still want us, you've got yourself a deal!" In my heart, I had known from the beginning we were going to sign with her. I knew it the minute she said we should go to God and pray about it. None of the other guys ever talked about God; they just talked about money. But Vicki said she wanted to tell people about Jesus, and that got me.

The rest, as they say, is history. GospoCentric bought that original tape from me for five thousand dollars, cleaned it up, did some new voice- and sound-over dubs, then put together an incredible master and released *Why We Sing* in June of 1993.

BREAKING OUT

By that time, demand for the new group, Kirk Franklin & the Family increased, and we were spending a lot of time on the road. I'd promised God that if He allowed me to do my minstry full time I would always give Him the glory and what belonged to Him (tithes and offerings). In January 1994, I was finally able to get a new car. Up until then I had been driving that raggedy little Fiero. But the word was already getting out, and people were calling us from all over the place. I was hearing, "Go here! Do that!" and I was being stretched to the point of snapping.

Before long, God blessed me with a new apartment. That was exciting, but with so many things happening at once, I really needed somebody to help me with the business affairs of the group.

My old friend from Grace Temple, Gerald Wright, was a capable businessman, plus he knew and loved gospel music like I did. So I asked him if he would come on as our manager. He really liked the idea, so he set up his new business, the Wright Group, and Kirk Franklin & the Family became his first client.

Today, of course, Gerald manages not only us but several other groups and artists we have worked with over the past five or six years—dancers, mimes, soloists, and groups.

I was seeing a lot of different young women at that time, but I was starting to think about finding the right one. You know, I think I was always looking for the right lady, but I just didn't know how to go about it. I kept jumping from one to the other, doing the things with women that seemed to satisfy other men but never satisfied me; I always left feeling empty. But I knew there had to be something better, and I wanted it.

The album started to move and really bless people. Its popularity started becoming more focused in the church community. We were getting more and more bookings in music halls and churches and other special venues. There were endless media interviews, and I was flying from New York to Los Angeles and all points in between. Everywhere I went, people were beginning to recognize me; that was an awesome responsibility.

As you might expect, being recognized is both good news and bad news. You're glad that people like your music, and you're honored and humbled that they want to see you and talk to you—but it gets to be a lot more work than anybody can really handle. And that was especially true for me—a kid who had grown up in the inner-city and hadn't anticipated anything like the success we were experiencing. Success brought out all my insecurities.

By December 1993, the song "Why We Sing" went to number one on the gospel music charts. At the end of the year it won two Stellar Awards, the top honor for gospel music. By March 1994 it went to number one on the Christian charts and won two Dove Awards in the contemporary Christian music market. That, I'm told, was a first for a gospel artist. We also received four GMWA (Gospel Music Workshop of America) awards in August 1994.

In December 1994, I got a call from Neily, our A&R contact at the record company in Los Angeles. A&R stands for "artists and repertoire," and people who work in that area have the closest contact with the musicians. She said, "Hey, Kirk, did you know that some of the R&B stations are starting to play your song?"

"Really?" I said. "No, I didn't know that. That's cool!" Gospel music doesn't usually get much air time on the R&B stations, so I was pleased but surprised. Most of all, I was just glad to know that the music was going to get some exposure in a wider audience.

But the next week Neily called again. "Kirk," she said, "it's a little bigger than I told you the last time I called."

"Oh yeah?" I said. "How much bigger?"

"'Why We Sing' has hit the R&B charts at number forty."

I nearly dropped the phone. I said, "You're kidding! We're on the R&B charts?"

She said, "Kirk, it's incredible, but you're on the R&B charts—and climbing!"

I couldn't believe it. But over the next few weeks they started playing our song on R&B stations at home, and the buzz was really going by this time. Before long the phone rang again, and this time it was Vicki Lataillade. She said, "Baby, we got to talk!"

Vicki was so excited. We had asked God to show us His will, but frankly, neither of us had anticipated this kind of success. Not on a first album! Vicki said she had been talking around and finding out what the stations all over the country were saying. She told me, "Kirk, they're saying this album could go gold!"

Sure enough, two weeks later, in mid-January 1994, *Why We Sing* went gold. But even before the album crossed over on the R&B stations, it had sold 250,000 units in the gospel market. Now, that's considered to be a good selling record in gospel and a blessing for our ministry; up to that time the average gospel album would sell 30,000 to 50,000 copies. If we had sold 50,000 units, we would have been thrilled.

Before we ever crossed over into the R&B charts, *Why We Sing* was already a big blessing with our home crowd. But something happened. Later, the writers at *Black Recording and Entertainment* magazine said in a cover story about us that it was "nothing short of a miracle."

When the urban stations started playing our song, it was a whole new thing for them. By all rights you would think that several months after an album was on the gospel music charts the album would be about ready to die. But all of a sudden it had popped up on the R&B stations, and they were pumping it like crazy.

So the album was born again! *Why We Sing* literally came back to life.

About that time we had released a Christmas album, and it was going very well too. When Vicki called we were putting the finishing touches on a major gospel release, *Whatcha Lookin' 4*, which had a slightly more progressive sound. We had already been in the studio doing the overdubs and remix recordings, but she said to put everything on hold.

"Baby," she said (Vicki always calls me baby!), "we can't put your new album out yet. It's too soon."

Whenever you do a new project you hate to wait. But Vicki said we needed to give the first album more time. With *Why We Sing* coming on strong in new markets, releasing another album at that time would not have been the wisest thing to do. So Vicki decided we needed to wait.

Not since Edwin Hawkins's hit song "Oh, Happy Day" back in 1972 had a gospel record taken the nation by storm the way that one did. The media were really into it too, saying stuff like, "This is the first time this kind of thing has happened in twenty years."

Over the years, a lot of gospel songs have hit the pop charts. Sister Rosetta Tharpe was really hot in the fifties, and the Clark Sisters hit it big with songs like "You Brought the Sunshine" in the eighties. In the early nineties the Winans and M. C. Hammer had chart-topping gospel hits. Obviously, some of those were crossover numbers and almost accidental hits. But "Why We Sing" was our title cut. It was outrageously popular, and I'm sure that helped pave the way for the even greater success of the *God's Property* album and the song "Stomp" in 1997.

THE UNEXPECTED

Looking at the exposure we were getting, I realized that even though GospoCentric Records had started out in Vicki Lataillade's garage, she wasn't starting empty handed. Going into it, Vicki had a ton of high-profile experience. She had spent her entire career in gospel music, and she had grown up working for some of the legends in the business.

When I met her, Vicki was widely known as one of the best promotional people in the record industry. She had handled Edwin Hawkins, André Crouch, Al Green, the Clark Sisters, Tramaine Hawkins, Vanessa Bell, Peabo Bryson, Take 6, Daryl Coley, Deniece Williams, the Tri-City Singers, and BeBe and CeCe Winans, among many others. She certainly wasn't a new kid on the block. Best of all, she believed in us, and just as she had promised, she was making sure the word got out about Kirk Franklin & the Family.

Both Vicki and I had paid our dues, working in and around the music business all those years. But it was as if this was what we had been in training for. God had planned it this way; He had just been holding it all back until the right moment, and suddenly all the hard knocks we had been through were paying off.

After fifteen years of coming up the hard way, people had the impression that we were an overnight success!

So much was happening. As the market was demanding more, more, more, Vicki decided she needed to hire an independent promotional team to help her handle all the inquiries. She had been all around the gospel market, but this was new territory for her, and she wanted to be sure we didn't let anything slip through the cracks. When the new team was on board, the first thing they said was, "Kirk needs to do a video."

So they started calling around and setting up plans to do an MTV-type video. I was just floating through all this; I couldn't believe any of it was happening. Meanwhile, our name was getting more well-known, not only in the music scene but with people back home. People who only knew Kirk Franklin & the Family from the gospel circuit were seeing us now in a whole new light.

We had been performing in churches for a long time, but suddenly we were being discovered by all these hip-hop kids. That was a trip.

About that time we were booked to perform at the Martin Luther King concert back home in Fort Worth. The King Concert is an annual event to celebrate Dr. King's birthday, and most years they would have from two to three thousand people in attendance—a good-sized crowd.

But in the meantime *Why We Sing* had gone gold, and the producers of the King Concert realized they were going to need more space. They were right; more than eight thousand people showed up for the concert.

After that things started to really pick up, and the favor of God started to show. But best of all, we were giving a strong witness of our faith every time we appeared in public and also striving to live a life before God offstage. Just when I was beginning to think we had seen it all, the producer of the *Arsenio* show called and wanted us to be on the show the same night that Louis Farrakhan was there. Talk about diversity!

It was all so fascinating! I was on my way to take my son to the doctor when I got the call. Monica Bacon of GospoCentric said, "Kirk, we just got a call from Arsenio Hall's producer, and he wants you on the show."

That was in February 1994, and I was surprised that anybody outside gospel music circles even knew our name. But here was the show that, at that time, was the hottest late-night talk show in Hollywood, calling to put us on nationwide television.

So we flew out to L. A., and Arsenio sent a limo to pick us up at the airport and drive us to Paramount Studios. But the minute we got there we saw all these security guards. Everywhere I looked there were black men in bow ties—obviously, Louis Farrakhan's people. And all around outside the gates, there were sign-toting people—both blacks and whites—protesting Farrakhan's appearance on TV.

When we got inside, Nation of Islam guards were at every door. But when our time came, we went out on stage and sang "He Can Handle It." We did a really jazzed-up rendition of the song, and it was well received. We enjoyed doing it, but I wanted to get that message out. The words say:

It really doesn't matter what you're going through.
I know that Jesus can work it out for you.
His yoke is easy, and His burden's light.
Just give it to Jesus, He'll make it all right.
He can handle it.
There's no doubt about my Savior,
I know He will deliver.
Whatever it is, He can handle it.

There's a simple but powerful message in those words, especially with Louis Farrakhan sitting there that night, pushing a very different message. We just wanted to let people know we were there to lift up the name of Jesus — because nobody can handle it like He can. Nobody!

What surprised me was that after the show Mr. Farrakhan came up to me and shook my hand and said, "Congratulations, Kirk. Just keep on lifting up the name of Jesus."

I hadn't expected that, but I understand that the Koran does say that Jesus is the Messiah. Even Muslims recognize Jesus as the Anointed One and a teacher of truth; they just don't recognize Him for who He is — the one and only Son of God. But the bad news is, that's the only thing that counts!

It breaks my heart to see the impact the Nation of

Islam is having on young black men today, because I see what's happening. Black men have not provided the leadership at home or in the community that they should have. They've fathered kids, abandoned their women, and run away from responsibility, and our kids are bitter and angry because they don't have a father figure in their lives.

Very cleverly, the Nation of Islam has come up with an answer. Unfortunately, it's the wrong answer. Jesus is the answer. He is the only way. But some churches have let the black community down, and that's one of the main reasons I do what I do—to call black men and black women back to Jesus. If they start there, through the music or through the invitation we offer in every concert, then that's at least a first step back to God, and that's where we have to be.

Almost immediately after Arsenio's show we started doing one national TV show after another. It seemed like we were constantly on airplanes flying off to some network studio for another show.

Most of the time, the hosts would clap politely and tell us they liked our sound. But when God's Property and I did *Live with Regis and Kathie Lee*, Kathie Lee Gifford was praising the Lord the whole time. That was really great, seeing a national talk-show host standing up for Jesus!

I'm not just a performer, of course; I'm also a fan. So I thought it was cool doing *Live from the Apollo* up in Harlem. It was exciting for us to be there, because I've heard so much about it, and I've enjoyed watching it on television for years. But I was really surprised at how small the theater is. Small building, small stage, big impact!

DOING THE CIRCUIT

One of the fascinating things about all the exposure we've had is seeing how different people react to what we do. Our main audience, the gospel fans, see our music as worship and praise. The mainstream secular market, however, sees it as black culture, not really as an art but as something vague like, "the voice of black music today."

Some of these people may like the beat, but they're not into the spirit of the music. I suspect the only reason we've been invited on some of these shows is the crossover appeal.

In those situations we would usually get the vibe, before and after the show, that neither we nor our message were really very important. It was like they were saying, "We just heard you were doing something different, and we wanted you to come. But as soon as the show's over, you're outta here!" There have been some occasions when the cars either didn't come or didn't come on time. And the accommodations at times were demeaning. After seeing the same treatment time after time, we realized that the level of respect for gospel music in our culture is still pretty low.

However, I have met several hosts who have a love for

the music and the message and have opened up their arms to us, and for that we are grateful.

But in our society, some people still think of gospel as yelling and screaming. For them, it's not an art; we just have to live with that. Fortunately, the attitude seems to be changing a little now, and, by the grace of God, I think the Family has had an impact on that. We have been blessed to bring many new ideas into the gospel scene, and there's a lot more art to it now than there used to be.

I still have to work very hard to always keep my eyes focused on the right things. It would have been easy when we were first starting out for me to start thinking I was Jesus' front man. But I have learned that it's not my job to change what people think or how they feel about this music. Our job is to do what we can with the gifts we have and let Jesus do His own thing.

Even though we don't do what we do for awards and status, God has blessed us, and in 1993 we won Stellar Awards for song of the year and best new artist. In 1994 our first album was named bestseller of the year by the National Association of Record Manufacturers; we also won the Bobby Jones Gospel Explosion Vision Award, four excellence awards, and two Gospel Music Association (GMA) Dove Awards for best album and best title song, and we were nominated for best gospel artist at the Soul Train Awards.

That's an incredible blessing for a bunch of young folks who came from nowhere. In 1995 and 1996 we were honored a dozen more times, including nominations for a

Church Boy

Grammy, three NAACP Image Awards, five Stellar Awards, a Soul Train Award, and a GMA Dove Award.

Whenever I go somewhere to receive an award or to participate in ceremonies for something the Family has done, I'm not going just for us but for a lot of other people too. What's important is the message.

And I also want to remember the ones who prepared the way for our success, including all those great gospel singers and musicians who came before us—many of whom never got the recognition they really deserved. So I honor them, and I try not to let my own success become a matter of personal pride because if I do I'm not real.

One of the good things about traveling is that I've accumulated a lot of miles, which allows me to upgrade to first class every now and then. Sometimes I am the only black person in first class. I think most people, including the airline employees, think I'm probably the relative of somebody who works for the airline.

Sometimes somebody will ask me, "So what do you do?"

I say, "I'm a musician."

They say, "Oh really? That's cool. What kind?"

And I say, "Gospel music."

Then they say, "Oh, I see." And that's the end of the conversation.

It's like they're thinking, *Uh-oh, this guy's going to try and get me saved!*

That's one reason I don't usually talk about what I do when we're traveling, because I don't want to seem to be that kind of Christian who's always shoving salvation in somebody's face. Jesus never forced His religion on anybody, and He didn't go around blowing His own horn.

He asked His boys, "Who do men say that I am?" (Luke 9:18). He didn't have to ask that. He already knew the answer. But He wanted them to figure it out for themselves. I'm always ready to give a witness for my faith, but I never want to hurt the cause of Christ by being overly aggressive with anybody.

If they want to know about Jesus, then we can talk. If they don't want to know, then I'm not going to force them to listen. But one thing is very clear, and I see it wherever I go. This country is hungry for something to believe in. People need hope, they need answers, and they need a Savior. And that's what our music is all about. Yes, I will even say, that's the reason why I sing, and it's why we're willing to travel nine months out of the year to share the love of Jesus. But we're not here to force it on anybody.

Expectations

(Part 3)

Tomorrow is a brand-new day,
All my sins have been washed away,
My hands look new, my life is free,
My heart is pure, I've been redeemed.

I've seen His face, touched His hands,
Finally now, I understand,
Why He saved a wretch, a wretch like me,
And by His blood I've been redeemed.

We ran the race, we kept the fight
We shed our blood for what was right,
We carried our cross through storm and rain.
Because of Christ, now we can say
We are conquerors, conquerors;
We are conquerors, conquerors.

No matter what we go through,
We are conquerors.
Lord, I'm gonna give my problems to You.
We are conquerors.

8

Conquerors

We recorded our second album in May 1994, and it proved to be a bigger blessing and a bigger challenge than any of us expected. The first album, *Why We Sing,* enjoyed so much musical success and received such great reviews that, in my flesh, I wasn't at all sure we could do it again. But as soon as *Whatcha Lookin' 4* was released, we could see that God was going to allow it to do as well or better than the first album.

Some people felt the music on the new album was more contemporary, more edgy, more sophisticated in some ways. If that's true, I don't think it was necessarily a conscious effort on our part. Some of our strongest critics, especially inside the church, said we had turned our backs on traditional gospel music and were just contemporary R&B artists exploiting Christian lyrics for the money. But that's not true.

The music we play today wasn't *designed.* We weren't trying to make any kind of statement; it just evolved naturally. It was a natural development and direction that we felt the music should take.

But I like to think that the growth and musical development are there because we were willing to let the music within us express itself. We weren't trying to imitate anybody's style or to make some kind of statement. We never pushed it. We just let the music take us wherever the Spirit led us and wherever the music wanted to go.

When the *God's Property* album came out in 1997, it was even more that way. In that one, God really gave me a chance to open up.

TRYING TO GET A LIFE

The *Whatcha Lookin' 4* album was a challenge for me because I was going through some personal and spiritual changes in my life.

I was twenty-four years old, and I knew I needed to get a grip on my life. I hated the stuff I had been into, and I hated the double life I had been living. But especially, I hated the loneliness and the sense of isolation, not having that special someone I could share my life with. I needed a wife, but I hadn't found the woman I wanted to marry.

So 1994 came and went, and I just kept up this crazy, hectic pace. We were doing some good stuff, traveling all the time, and suddenly a lot more people knew who we were. Word was getting out that God was allowing something new to happen in gospel music. But it was a crazy time for me personally. I had this new popularity, and all that comes with it, but I was still empty inside. By 1995, I was wrestling with those things while the music was really taking off.

We began doing what felt like hundreds of radio and TV

shows. We were on *Good Morning, America* and CNN's *Showbiz Today*, and we were featured on *Headline News* and *Prime Time News* segments. You name it, we've been there. We have even done the Letterman show twice.

We've been flown to national broadcasts on private jets, picked up by chauffeurs and private limos, been interviewed by *USA Today* and *The New York Times*, and had stories and interviews appear on all the major wire services and hundreds of local newspapers and monthly magazines.

I was featured in *Ebony*, and that helped our visibility, not only with the mainstream black audience, but with the general market as well. My picture appeared on the cover of the August 1997 issue of the inspirational magazine *Guideposts*, which carried my article about the fall during our Memphis concert. Before that I was on the covers of two or three other Christian magazines. Through these outlets there's almost no segment of the population we haven't reached in some way.

So far, according to our publicists at GospoCentric who keep track of these things, we've done more than two dozen appearances on network television and have been featured on ten national TV programs, thirty local TV specials, and fifty radio features, and we've appeared in one hundred major newspaper articles and thirty national magazine articles, including *Billboard, USA Today, People* magazine, *Jet, Vibe, Cash Box, Rolling Stone, CCM, Gavin, Urban Network, R&B, HITS,* and *Entertainment Weekly.*

I was on CNN twice before I fell in Memphis and

twice afterward, and all of that coverage has helped give the group and our albums more exposure than we could ever have imagined. At one point, *USA Today* wrote that our success "represents a new day in gospel music." The article said that since the accident in Memphis I had become "gospel music's biggest star." Now, I know that kind of stuff can go to a young man's head. But I do not intend on letting it. I'm so busy working on *me* that I don't have time to focus on all the hype.

I never want to let myself get into the mold of thinking that I'm more than I am. For one thing, I know God is calling the church to repentance today, at this very minute. We are trying to do something with a highly visible and highly audible impact, but it's not my message; it's His. And to be totally honest, it's not really my music. God put all that stuff inside me that would allow us to bring forth the message He wanted to get out.

God gave me a ministry of music and schooled me in it from the age of four. He put me through some heavy-duty stuff so that, when the time came, I'd be able to use those gifts to minister to people's hearts and to touch people who needed a word of encouragement. That's what Kirk Franklin & the Family is all about. That's why we sing. It's not us; it's Him.

IN THE SPOTLIGHT

The song "Why We Sing" and its accompanying album changed my life. As I said earlier, 1995 was a very challenging year in many ways, both good and bad; but the success of the album helped to bring a lot of things in my life into sharper focus—things I don't think I ever really understood until that time. When we released *Whatcha Lookin' 4* later that year, the success of the new album just took everything to a higher level.

Whatcha Lookin' 4 hit *Billboard's* Top 200 chart at number 23, the R&B chart at number 5, and both the video and the contemporary Christian charts at number 1. That was the highest breakout ranking of any gospel album in history, and we were totally blessed by it.

So much was happening so fast. For the first time we had a chance to perform overseas. We went to Frankfurt, Germany, and performed for a large mixed crowd of Germans and Americans, blacks and whites, and it was such a blessing to go there. We've been to the Bahamas many times now as well as to Barbados and London; we also did a big concert in Birmingham, England, in 1997—not to mention, of course, touring virtually every major city in the United States over the past three years.

The business end is not my strength. I enjoy getting onstage and becoming one with the people. I enjoy getting a chance to make an audience feel what I feel. But the Fort Worth boy inside of me is always aware of the risks and the temptations of this business, and I have made it a matter of constant prayer not to be sucked in by the hype.

With all the things we've done and the places I've been, I've worked very hard not to let ego or pride get in the way of the message. I've focused on this so much that sometimes when it's appropriate to talk about the way it all happened, either for a newspaper story, a TV interview, or even for this book, I find it very hard to open up. There's a part of me that's afraid to get into it, not to mention the fact that sometimes it's just hard to remember!

My constant prayer is that I can stay honest and humble before God so I won't have to focus on these things and instead can just be faithful and use the talents and the opportunities I've been given to the glory of God. People tell me I can't afford to overlook the PR aspect because celebrity and commercial success help us get the music out to the audience we want to reach. But I prefer to leave that to people who know more about it. I'm doing my best to focus my energies on the music and message God gave me.

I heard this illustration not long ago, and maybe it will help explain what I'm trying to say. There's a point when natural instinct and musical training just take over so that the consciousness of doing it actually disappears. It's the same thing for professional athletes. If a football running back, for example, concentrates on his moves and starts thinking about what he's supposed to do to be a great runner, he probably won't get the job done. But if he just lets go and lets his talent loose, then he becomes the athlete he was born to be. That's how it ought to work.

If I—or the members of the Family—allow ourselves to concentrate on all the media hype and all the Hollywood stuff, or if we start thinking about how we play the game, we'll soon lose our focus. So when we go out on stage to perform we just rest in what God has given us. At some point it's like there's this audible click, and we become "Kirk Franklin & the Family." God's in control, the music starts to work, and then we just do what we do best.

How else can I explain the Grammys and Stellars and Image Awards? How do I account for three sold-out nationwide tours, three platinum albums, and a gold Christmas album? But, you know, even as I say that, it's hard for me to talk about those things. There are a lot of people who already think I've let the success go to my head. A lot of people—especially in the church—have said that I'm starting to believe my own press. But I don't think that's the case, and I also say that I work very hard to keep my head on straight.

Besides that, working with those fifteen beautiful, talented, outspoken singers called the Family, I'm constantly surrounded by people who do a pretty good job of making sure none of the stuff goes to my head! They've been there through all the hype and they remember me before we made the first nickel. And, believe me, they keep me humble!

There are stories that appear in print now and then that could easily make a guy think he's somebody special. If I'm not careful, I could find myself looking in the mirror someday and saying, "Yeah, that's right. I am all that!" But I never want—and I honestly pray—that day will never come.

That's not what I'm in it for. Everybody in the Family and everybody in the Franklin family—meaning my wife,

Tammy, and the kids—have been told to remind me of who I am. And if it ever looks like I'm crossing the line and falling for all the hype, then I expect them to grab me and say, "Hey, Kirk. Chill, brother!"

A CHANGE OF VIEW

My *radicalness,* if there's such a word, hasn't created as much controversy as you might think it would. I mean, with some of the things we do onstage—coming out with a group like God's Property and dancing around out there or rolling across the stage praising the Lord like I do— you'd think the traditional church would have boycotted me. But it hasn't, and I'm glad for that.

I do a disclaimer at the beginning of every concert. A few years ago it was like an apology, asking people to be patient with us and not to judge us until they heard what we had to say. Then for a while it was not so much an apology as an explanation. But now, after we've seen what God is doing in the lives of young people through this music, it's more like a seat-belt warning. "Okay, people, buckle up. Let's get our praise on!"

What we give young people is hope. We let them know they're not alone and that there are others who feel the way they do. We know the world is chewing them up. Gangs are sucking them in. Sex and AIDS and sexually transmitted diseases are killing them and ruining their lives. In the face of all that stuff, our music is there to say, "Don't give up. God can help!"

Church Boy

Both these groups, Kirk Franklin & the Family and God's Property, are trying to take our young people back to where they belong. We want to save lives, not lose them. We have all been there ourselves. We know the risks. Some of the young people who are singing with God's Property today were gang-bangers just a couple of years ago. So they know what that kind of life is like, and they have found out that Jesus has a better answer. That's the answer we want to give them. We want to share our hope.

If some of the preachers and youth ministers in the local churches can't see what's happening to their kids, then they've got to be blind. Sometimes hard-nosed traditionalists are blinded by their beliefs so that they can't see that reality. Maybe they don't even want to admit the truth of what's happening out there or who's ultimately responsible for it. The church hasn't always been there for those young people. The only thing those hard-nosed traditionalists can see is that these musicians are really wild and seem pretty far out for gospel singers.

Ever since that first meeting back in 1992 when we laid out the basic outlines of the Family, we've been concerned about the legalism in the church. We've been hurt by it, but I can honestly say it's a lot better today than it was five years ago.

Those who live by rigid legalism may not be able to see the obvious. And too often they can't even see how their attitudes are driving young people out of the church and into the streets and the gangs and the clubs. But sooner or later there has to be a reality check.

When they say, "It's not what I'm used to and I don't like it, so I'm not having it in my church," what they're actually saying is, "I don't want to keep these kids in the house of God if that's the kind of music they want to hear. So I'm not having them here in my church anymore." Rather than seeing what the music can do for the hearts and minds of their kids, they toss them out the door and give them up to the world.

Any minister who loves God ought to rejoice to see young people praising the name of Jesus and focusing their eyes on Him instead of the cheap imitations the world is offering. Instead of saying, "I'm not having that in my church," they need to be singing with us at the top of their lungs, "Go Jesus, go Jesus, go!"

God knows our motives. He has really sheltered us. And my relationship with the Family is very important in helping me keep my focus. Those men and women know me like nobody else, and they remember me when. They keep me accountable.

Here's just one example: When we were in Oklahoma City on tour in mid-1997, I overheard David Mann telling somebody, "Yeah, I love him, but I've known him for thirteen years. I've known him since he was a snot-nosed kid." I laughed at that, but that's how it should be. They love me, but they also remind me who I am and where I came from.

What has always been a concern for me—and for a time I think it discouraged me from doing some of the things I really wanted to do—was that I never wanted to do anything that might screw up whatever God was doing through our music. It was very evident that He was doing something. And I was so scared, thinking, *I'm going to do something and blow this.*

Not that I was doing so much wrong in general, but my lifestyle and the casual promiscuity that seems to come along with this crazy business was just killing me. A lot of people didn't know about it at the time; either they didn't think about it, didn't consider it, or just didn't care. But my flesh was killing me.

There was never a time when I got caught up in it and thought I was pulling something over on anybody. And there was never a time when I got focused in on the money or the awards or the media hype or any of that stuff. I just didn't want to blow it.

What made it worse was that nobody around me was saying, "Kirk, you gotta get a grip on this, and stop it now!" People were pulling on me. Girls would say, "Kirk, I don't want anything; let's just watch TV and hold hands." They'd say they wanted to do whatever I wanted to do, except there was always this compromise and sudden change of attitude when we were alone together.

That stuff wasn't happening because that's what I wanted. It was happening because I thought that's just the way it was. A lot of the pastors and preachers and music leaders I had known were doing it. And I honestly thought for a time that that's what you were supposed to do.

Consequently, I misinterpreted sex for love. I thought

sex was the main thing—until later when I realized how empty I was inside. And that awareness was the first step toward emotional and spiritual healing.

The hype, the media, and all the pomp and circumstance never did shake me. What was awesome for me wasn't just the success. It wasn't that I was suddenly able to go into the store and buy whatever I wanted or needed. What blew me away was the awareness that suddenly I could start helping other people through my financial blessings.

I always loved doing that, even when I was going to Jolly Time and had a little bit of change in my pocket. I mean, I was making a hundred dollars a month at Mount Rose, so I could pay my friends' way into the skating rink. Of course, they weren't really my friends. They were just hanging out with me on Saturday nights. But I enjoyed doing something for other people, even then.

By January 1995 I knew I couldn't go on with the life I was leading. I didn't want to hurt God, and I knew I'd already been doing that to some degree. Things were going much too fast, and I didn't want to let them go any further. So I knew I had to make some changes.

I believe that all things work together for the good of those who love the Lord, and now that I'm a little older and a little bit wiser, I think that what I went through can give me a stronger witness with some of the young people I'm talking to in my music. My failures and my inability to resist the temptations I fell into are the proof that I've been there. But, thank God, today I've been set free. And if I did it, you can too!

Today I use my own struggles to talk to young men. I say, "Listen, young man. Don't do it! Respect yourself, respect that young woman, respect your mama, and remember the values she tried to teach you."

Staying clean, staying pure — it's not just the right thing to do, it's the best thing because it's what God wants from you.

I can say to that young woman out there, "Stop now. Turn it over to Jesus. Do it for Him, and you do it for yourself at the same time."

And then I say, "Listen to me, young man. I'm telling you the truth because I've been there, and I regret it more than I can say." Some of those young men and women will listen to me. They know I'm not lying.

SOMEONE SPECIAL

God allowed me to go through it all. Then, in the midst of His taking my music ministry to another level, He strategically put Tammy back in my life. I was just eighteen when I first met Tammy. She had grown up in Arlington, Texas, not far from where I lived. I saw her exactly once, but something locked in my mind. I knew she was special.

I met her again in 1992 through her cousin Titia, who at the time was dating someone who was helping me on the *Why We Sing* demo. Titia invited Tammy to come to the recording of the demo. We started dating and would see or talk to each other almost every day until she and her group moved to Minneapolis to pursue a career in R&B music.

We tried to maintain a long-distance relationship but I didn't have a record contract yet, so I didn't have the means to see her, nor did she have the means to come to Texas.

We developed a good friendship but, because of the distance, it was difficult to pursue the relationship. We began seeing other people but would keep in touch. The distance was hard, and soon it was painful to speak to each other because we had feelings we could not act on. There was a time I would not return her phone calls because conversation would stir up those feelings. So she stopped calling, but would leave a message from time to time.

Then one day in 1995, right when I knew I needed to get some things settled between God and me, Tammy came back into my life. Out of the blue, she called and left a message on my machine.

She said, "Hi, Kirk. This is Tammy, and I just wanted to see how you're doing. But Kirk, this is the last time I'm leaving a message. You haven't returned any of my calls, and if you don't return this one I'm not going to call back anymore." She left her number and hung up, and that was it.

I called her back. Coincidentally, she was going to be in Detroit the same time I was to see her family, who had been relocated from Texas.

I made it a point to call her when we arrived. I spent some time with her and her family in Detroit, and it was really nice. She was more beautiful than I remembered. She wasn't pushy and aggressive like so many girls I knew. She was quieter, cuter, cooler, and more natural. She was comfortable to be with, and I liked that.

Church Boy

She flew with me for a concert in Oakland, California, and we had a chance to talk about who we were inside and what we were really looking for in all this. I had been dating another girl off and on the past year and a half, but I could see it wasn't going to turn into anything. I wanted somebody who loved the Lord and the church as much as I did, but I was trying to make that girl into what I thought she should be. It wasn't fair to her, and it wasn't working.

So when Tammy came back into my life, I thought it was good timing for making some changes. After the Oakland performance I had to go down to Los Angeles, and she came with me. While we were there I asked her to be my girlfriend. And that Sunday morning we went to church with a friend of mine.

A NEW REALM

Ever since I was a baby, Gertrude had been putting stuff in me to create a fear of God—a reverence for God and a profound respect for the authority of God. So that was working.

I have always been a Jesus freak. I've always been a lover of God, even when I was embarrassed around people. When I was put up on this platform, that didn't change. Things would start coming at me sometimes that I wasn't strong enough to push off. When they would come, sometimes I would accept them. But I wanted to change.

I remember how I had felt just a few months earlier when

I was on my way to San Diego for the national convention of the National Association of Record Manufacturers. It's a very big, very important convention for people in this business. But on the way to the airport I was feeling really low. I had spent the weekend with a girl who didn't mean anything to me. She had just flown out to hang around with me, and as I headed toward San Diego I wondered why I had let myself get into that situation.

At one point I said to Jessie Hurst, my buddy and road manager, "Jessie, I'm tired of it. I'm sick and tired of this lifestyle."

Jessie said, "Kirk, I know what you're saying. You've said it before. But what are you going to do about it?"

I said, "Man, I wish I could just settle down and find that one special person I'd like to marry."

Jessie said, "I hear you talking about people, Kirk, and I know most of the women you go out with. But nobody you talk about ever seems to make you happy. Isn't there anybody you really like?"

I thought for a minute and said, "There's this girl I met one time back in 1988. We dated for a while back in 1992, then she left, and that's about the only girl I can honestly say I ever really liked."

That girl was Tammy.

Nothing more was said about it then. But we flew out to San Diego for the convention, and while I was there I really thought about all that and prayed about it. When I got back to Los Angeles, I went to see a pastor friend who lives there, and I said, "Man, I'm really tired of this lifestyle. I'm sick and tired of being by myself. Tired of being single and tired of dating, because it's doing nothing but just draining me."

My friend knew what I was saying. Like Jessie, he had heard it all before too. I continued unloading on him for a while and said what was in my heart, "I know God is not going to send me anybody with the lifestyle I have right now. He's not going to send me anybody I can hurt. I know what I've got to do, and it's not going to be easy. But I've got to stop messing around and practice abstinence until God puts that special person in my life."

Later that afternoon I called the young lady I was dating and said we had to stop. From that moment on I was committed to getting all that stuff under control and, with God's help, cleaning up my act in every area.

God had put Tammy back into my life in such a miraculous way. I had always felt that there was something very special about Tammy. She was unique. Everything about her was godly—her heart, her spirit, and her mind. The instant I saw her, I knew this was it. I knew I wanted our relationship to be permanent. I wanted to spend the rest of my life with her. About a month later, I asked her to be my wife, and when she said yes, it was the best day of my life. Of all my many blessings, that was the greatest.

I honestly believe that God used Tammy to usher me into a new realm, a new opportunity for God's purposes in my life. We both knew our love was special, so we made sure our wedding was special too.

When we finally had the ceremony on January 20, 1996, I couldn't believe it was really happening. Tammy and her mother planned an absolutely beautiful wedding. There were flowers, music, decorations. Tammy's wedding dress was awesome, and even the groomsmen looked good in their black tuxedos!

All our close friends and family were there, and when Tammy and I exchanged wedding vows, we also exchanged vows of love and faithfulness with our children. I pledged to love and care for her daughter, Carrington, and Tammy made the same kind of vow to my son, Kerrion. We left nothing out, because we both knew this was for real, and it was for life.

MAKING SENSE OF IT

Later, when we compared notes on how the whole thing started and how we fell in love in the first place, it was cool to find out that Tammy had been going through a lot of the same emotions that I was feeling at the time. Whenever she would think about getting married and settling down, she says my name always seemed to come up, out of the blue. She would hear something about me, or somebody would mention my name. One time her mother asked, "Tammy, whatever happened to that young man you were seeing down in Texas?" Things like that happened so often she started to think that maybe it wasn't just coincidence.

There was one particular guy she knew during this

time who seemed to go out of his way to keep her posted on all the negative things he could come up with about me. Tammy says it was like he was working overtime telling her awful stuff, most of which wasn't even true. She realized it was probably the enemy trying to cloud her mind with negative feelings for the man she might be interested in marrying. But, ironically, the more this guy talked trash to her, the more she thought about me and worried about me. He was trying to make himself look better, but in the end he only made me look better.

Because of her own musical career and the temptations she'd been exposed to, Tammy knew what I had been going through. She knew I was traveling too fast, doing too much, seeing too much of the world, and she realized that God couldn't use me in that condition. But the spiritual part was that she was feeling really burned out about her own relationships at that time and Tammy was asking herself, "Is this all there is? Is this what it's really all about?"

Little did we know that when I returned her call we both were coming into what we had been praying for. She was tired of compromising her faith to sing R&B, and she didn't want to portray a negative image for her daughter, Carrington. She was fed up with dating, and wanted to truly live for the Lord. We feel her phone call to me was totally God, because she was becoming anti-relationships. When I called it wasn't magical or anything. She was still skeptical. But it was the first step.

Like me, Tammy grew up in the church, singing in the

choir, and even after she got involved with R&B music, she still had a love for God. The group she sang with, Ashanti, was into empowerment for women—saying "You can do it!" and stuff like that. But in the R&B world, the message didn't mean very much. They were three attractive young women, and the music industry demanded that everything they did had to be suggestive and sexy—the sexier the better—and that was hard for Tammy.

Because she had to go through all that, I think she probably understood my situation better than most wives in this business. Today she understands and supports me, and she doesn't see my ministry as just another job. But I know it's been hard for her to see me spending so much time on the road. Tammy has worked hard to make our home a special place—a private place where we can just relax and enjoy our children. But up until the fall of 1997, it was almost impossible to have as much time at home as we would have liked. That's changing now, thank goodness, and we've been able to take some time off to relax and have fun together. That's been an incredible blessing for both of us.

Tammy prayed that God would give our new baby, Kennedy, a special relationship with her daddy, and it's so rewarding for me to see how God is answering her prayers. I never knew my own father, and I don't want to be an absentee father for my kids. Our children are so special and so very precious to me. Spending time with Tammy and the kids has given me a joy and a sense of accomplishment like nothing I've ever known. No wonder everybody's into family values these days. They're right. If God's at the center of it, there's no greater happiness than spending time with your family.

In some of the stories that came out after the accident in Memphis in November 1996, people were saying it was the fall that straightened me out. Honestly, I don't believe that the fall had anything to do with any of that, except this: The fall was just God's way of speeding up the growing up process that was taking place. I was already on my way. But it was like stepping on the accelerator. The fall put all those things into high gear.

Whether I'm living high on the hill or down in the projects, I'm cool, so long as God is leading me every step of the way. But I will say this: What the accident did for me was take me from age twenty-six to age forty in one day. You know what I'm saying?

It sped up the process I was already on. I was running as fast as I could to get things right, to get my walk with the Lord back in step, but suddenly God stepped in and took it all on Himself. I didn't have to do it in my strength because He was entirely capable of doing it in His strength. He used the fall in Memphis to teach me that lesson.

I have been quoted in several publications for something I said about the fall's impact on my life. I said I didn't really appreciate my ministry until I saw it in the light of that dark night in Memphis. Realizing I could have lost it all, I suddenly appreciated what I have in an all new way.

I could have died, or I could have wound up a vegetable. In five short years I had gone from a kid who borrowed five grand to make a demo tape to an international celebrity, but somehow the surprise and suddenness of it eclipsed the full force of the transformation. It was like giving a four-year-old a diamond. I didn't know what I had.

When you have responsibility and the ear of the people but you don't realize the power and the impact of your position, you don't know what you've got. I have to be careful about saying this because some people have misconstrued it and tried to imply that before Memphis I didn't love God, that I wasn't saved, or maybe that I didn't even believe what I was saying. But the fall had nothing to do with my not loving God. That would be an easy thing to say, and it might have made good press, but I'm glad to say that's not the case.

Before Memphis I was on my way. I was working on everything about me, and I was still striving to grow closer to God. But after Memphis, it was like, Let's don't *work* on it anymore; let's just *do* it. You know? Let's not *work* on being God's man; let's just get rid of those weights holding us down. Let's *be* God's man.

I never graduated from high school. I never had the privilege of walking across the stage. But Memphis was my graduation. That was me walking across the stage and getting my diploma. It was my battle scar. It was my coming of age.

I was off the tour from the first of November until the

twenty-sixth of December that year, but I was still doing something. I flew home on Tuesday, November 15, with strict orders from the doctors to stay in bed, take my medication, and not do anything that would raise my blood pressure. But the very next Sunday I was in church preaching. I knew God had given me an opportunity. He had done what I knew in my spirit He was going to do that night. He let something happen that would change our lives forever.

Altogether, I eventually took six weeks off the tour, and that was great because it was over the Christmas holidays. But we reprogrammed all the tour dates that had been canceled after the accident and went back on the road the last week of December 1996.

We picked up with New Orleans and made the full circuit, playing to crowds of from five to ten thousand people everywhere we stopped. Since that time God has prospered our ministry, our music, and our message in a way no one on earth could have anticipated. And He has done a work in me that has truly made me a new man in Christ.

When I cannot hear the sparrow sing
And I cannot feel a melody,
There's a secret place
That's full of grace.

There's a blessing in the storm;
Help me sing it!
There's a blessing in the storm.

When the sickness won't leave my body
And the pain just won't leave my soul,
I get on my knees
And say, "Jesus, please!"

There's a blessing in the storm;
Help me sing it!
There's a blessing in the storm.

When I cannot seem to love again
And my burdens seem to never end,
I get on my knees
And say, "Jesus, please!"

There's a blessing in the storm;
Help me sing it!
There's a blessing in the storm.

9

A Blessing in the Storm

here has been so much drama in my life the last few years—the music, the traveling, TV and radio appearances, the various awards and recognition of what God has accomplished with us, not to mention the fall. And along with all of that, getting married, and then the new baby coming along, plus all the business aspects of what we do. Being on the road as much as I've been the last three years, I've had very little time to myself.

Tammy and I sometimes have had to go months before we could slow down enough to take time out for ourselves, but there is a price to pay for this kind of ministry. You simply don't get time to focus on things when you're running this fast.

Just sitting down to work on this book has been a major adjustment for me, but it's also been one of the first times I've had time to sit back and reflect on what it all means. And it's been a learning experience.

I can honestly say I am not a media person, because I see how living in the spotlight takes over people's lives. The spotlight can get pretty hot, and the media can be pretty cold. I know if that's where I put my hopes, sooner or later I'll be very, very disappointed. So I work at keeping my focus on other things.

I remember watching Tiger Woods on TV one afternoon. Of course, Tiger's a great golfer and a young man who has taken an important first step for black athletes. He won several huge tournaments back to back and proved that golf can be as much a black man's game as anybody's. But he didn't win that day, and I noticed that the media's vibe was very different from what it had been just a few weeks earlier. The vibe was different because Tiger didn't win.

When he had won at Augusta and then later at the Byron Nelson Tournament, the reporters were all saying he was the best to ever play the game. But the minute he dropped back in the pack at the next couple of tournaments, those same reporters were gone, chasing some other celebrity. So much for fame.

But maybe that's only fair. After all, modern society is about winners. But not everybody who's a winner in the eyes of men is a winner in life. Not everybody who's being chased by the media and not everybody who's in the spotlight today will necessarily be the real winner when all is said and done.

In fact, the guy who came in last may be the real winner.

The guy who got the trophy and all the media attention may have cheated. Maybe he was on steroids or cheating on his wife or playing fast and loose with his income tax. And maybe the guy who came in last wasn't in the winner's spotlight because he wasn't on drugs. Or maybe he was up late helping his daughter with her homework. Maybe he was spending time helping somebody else instead of helping himself. So who's the real winner?

I decided a long time ago that the only way I could stay right with God was to limit what I do with the media. Not my sanity, not my emotions, not my mentality, but my salvation. I know people who would sell their soul for good press, but I won't do that. As much as we want to get the message out, there are some things more important to me than good press.

FINISHING STRONG

When I finish the race, the relationship that will mean the most to me will be my relationship with God. After that, God expects me to hold up my wife and children, to be there for them, to love and bless them and give them the best of my love.

Yes, I do have a ministry of music, and I do love to perform and touch people with it. But I realize that in the big picture I can't allow that work to take me away from my first responsibility to God and my family.

I'm hard on myself already for little things, for comments I may make to the mailman or to a salesclerk. I'm always checking myself because I never want to come across wrong. I never want to hurt anybody or seem arrogant or proud. I mean, I've been up and I've been down, and I've met some rats at both ends. But I never want to be like that. I don't want to lose my perspective or my ability to stay focused on the things that matter most.

I'm glad to say that everybody in the Family agrees with me on this; they feel the way I do about it. We all struggle with time and work and family pressures, but we have a much better idea today than we did a couple of years ago about what really counts.

I've said this before, and I'll say it again. That fall in Memphis in 1996 wasn't just my fall. It was the Family's fall too. It was a fall for all of us.

It was everybody's fall because it opened our eyes to some things we hadn't thought about until that night. For example, right before Memphis they loved me, and we're very close as a group of performers and friends; but when you've been around somebody for so long you start to take a lot of things for granted. Just like me. I was taking each day for granted.

Sometimes you take God's love and His grace for granted. But Memphis taught us not to take anybody or anyplace or anything for granted. It taught us to appreciate each day and everything in it in a way we never had before—the good stuff and the bad stuff, the easy days and the hard ones. The sunshine, the rain, and even the storms in our lives. Suddenly everything had value that had just been business up until then. We saw life and all that it has to offer with new eyes, because life is both good and bad.

As I said earlier, Memphis was my graduation. I didn't get a chance to graduate from high school. A lot of other things got in the way, and I never did walk across that stage in Fort Worth. Instead, I walked across a stage in Memphis and that's where I got not only my diploma but my education.

When David Mann told me later what I said while I was lying there in blood—"Speak, Lord! Give me a word!"—that told me something I really needed to hear. It showed me where my heart was. You know how the enemy is. The enemy makes you doubt yourself in so many ways. He says, "Ah, man, you're not really in the will. You're not humble; you're just in it for the money!"

But knowing that I was talking to God at that moment helped me to know that, even lying there in a semiconscious state, absolutely helpless, I was looking to God for a word. You see, that's my personal commitment, to never let the enemy take my joy away from me, to never let him steal my peace. He'll do it if I let him. He's always trying. So now I say, don't let the devil steal your glory.

When he fights me now it's not about women or money or power. He fights me in the little secret places. He's always whispering doubts and fears and trying to weaken my resolve. But he's out of his league because this isn't just my ministry. It's God's.

For the Family and my family and for all of us, Memphis was a wake-up call. For one thing, when I fell, everybody had to go home, and there was no work for the next six weeks. It was like being laid off a job and having no pay. Nobody was making anything, and if I hadn't recuperated it might have all been over right there that night.

I wouldn't say we were a different group when we went back out on the road that December, but I think that, spiritually and musically, we were all a little hungrier and there was a little more sense of purpose to what we did.

I understand better now what the fall was for. The fall wasn't for the stuff onstage; the fall was for the stuff offstage. Because the stuff offstage is what we're judged by. I'm not judged by that stuff onstage. Anybody can put a suit on and do that. There's a lot of talented heathens out there. But that's not what gets God's attention.

He has His eye on the stuff offstage, and when we get the personal and private stuff straightened out and start living right every day, then He gets excited about what we're doing. I truly believe that.

The stuff God cares about is the stuff at the house, the stuff with the kids, the stuff when you're driving home from the studio at 1:30 in the morning and instead of going straight home you know there are opportunities to take the next exit and go down that side street and go to that certain house where the devil would be glad to lure you in.

That's when it counts, when you are accountable and honest and you turn your back on those temptations because you love God more than you love this world. When you no longer have any interest in calling up that old girlfriend or stopping by the dirty video place or always just looking for that little something on the side like so many people are doing these days.

That's the stuff. That's what God cares about. How are

you walking when it's time to be completely transparent about all that? I've been there. I know what it's like to be onstage, performing God's music and thinking about who I'll be going home with that night. But never again. Now I go home to my wife, because to truly love and serve God is to love her.

SHAKING THE RAFTERS

I don't want people to read this book and think that I'm just a carnal Christian, but at the same time I want to be honest and real. I'm not proud of where I've been, what I've done, or who I was at one time. My past still troubles me today, and I wish it had never happened. There were times when my sexual identity dictated all those things— who I was, what I did, and where I went. But no more. God is putting it all behind me day by day.

The hardest part of this for me, however, is not so much that I failed, but that at this moment there are people in churches all across this nation, in every city and town, who are still caught up in that lifestyle of promiscuity, that compromise with sin, and they're pretending it doesn't matter at all.

Well, I'm here to tell you, my friend, it does matter. I know from my own experience that it matters. It matters a lot. And Jesus Christ is saying to you today, whoever you are, wherever you are, no matter how successful you've been, that you had better give it up right now and get right with God right now, while you still can.

I want to shake the church with this book. I want to shake every pastor who's compromising with sin. I want to shake every deacon and elder who's looking the other way while sin crawls through the doors of that church every Sunday morning. I want to shake the world and those in it to say, "Truly listen to the message."

I want to shake the mothers and fathers who pretend they don't know what their boys and girls are doing out there every night, sleeping around, using drugs, messing with stuff that will kill them and rob them of their joy. And I want to shake up every one of those young people with this book and with every lyric I write.

I'll shake the rafters if I have to and say: "Look, brother! You gotta get right with God right now! Please, for Christ's sake and for your own sake, get your eyes back where they belong, while there's still time!"

I'll say, "Satan has laid his hooks into you, young person, and you're not free. You talk about slavery and you talk about your rights and you talk about how somebody's holding you down. But look here, boo: *It's you!* You're holding yourself down with your addiction to sin.

"Unless you give it up right now and get right with God right now, you've let the enemy put his handcuffs back on your wrists. Actually, you put them on yourself, so the devil did it with your help. And you've made yourself a slave to sin. Young man, you better get right, right now. Young woman, young person, do it now while you can."

I want every young person, every mother and father,

every grandparent and pastor and friend to understand that I was like that myself at one time, and I'm still dying daily. But I wasn't doing those things because I wanted to; I was doing them because I just thought that's the way it was. Then, when I found out that it doesn't have to be that way, I was already in so deep it took me years to break free and get out of that prison of sin.

It breaks my heart to realize it took me nearly ten years to break out.

I also want to get into this book how important my wife is to me. I call Tammy my sanity. And Jessie Hurst—the guy who jumped down into the pit to get me when I fell in Memphis—Jessie's my covering. We've been together a long time. And Gerald Wright, my business manager, is my friend, in the sense that a true friend is somebody who is always there for you and always cares.

Every now and then you have to get back on track when you have a lot of things shoved in your face. When you love God, you have no choice but to be accountable. Tammy and the Family, all fifteen of them, help me do that. They know me, they stand with me, but they remind me of my word and my witness whenever I need a little push. I love them for that and for many other things.

I want to get very vocal about the way I was raised because I know I'm not the only one. Sometimes onstage, without any rehearsal or any deliberate plan to do it, I feel the impulse to just share my heart about those things.

I was born out of wedlock to a mother who would have aborted me if a godly aunt hadn't intervened. I grew up on the poor side of town and was taunted and teased and beat on as long as I can remember. But God was there for me. He didn't let me go. And that's where I am.

I know that's what I have to say because that auditorium or theater is filled with people who know just what I'm talking about. Either they've been there or they know somebody who has, and they need to know that they can beat it. They don't have to live like that because Jesus can set them free.

That's where I am. Too often we put on these suits and ties and preach to people about the grace of God—and "Oh, isn't it wonderful!"—before the people have had a chance to get transparent and honest about who they are. They listen to all those sermons and sing all the uplifting hymns, and they never come to grips with the deadly claws wrapped around their hearts.

They go home and battle with pornography, drugs, alcohol, adultery, and all these other things because they don't have anywhere to go and unload that stuff. They're crying out, "Can't anybody hear me? Can't anybody help me without judging me? Is anybody else going through this junk I'm going through?"

The answer is, "Yes, Jesus knows. He hears your cry, and He loves you more than you'll ever know."

I want to help get that message out there, and one of the newest things we're doing now is making plans for a convention called "Nu Nation." We're going to try to put on a major event every summer, from the year 2000 on, and it's going to be a conference for young people from all over the country. It's going to be an incredible buildup. I can't wait!

I want to give people—young and old—a format, a place where they can say, "Hey, I got some junk! Can we talk about it?" And when they leave that place they can honestly say they've been helped, they've been loved, and they'll know that somebody cares for them. We're talking about organizing this thing so that people can get serious help and support from other people who've been there. I'm thinking about doing a "Nu Nation" website on the Internet where people can log on and chat with others who've found some answers. I think there will be many, many ways we can touch people and give them some hope.

You know, there's another guy out there trying to raise up a nation, and he'll do it if we turn our eyes and look away from God. But God is saying we've got to give the young people better choices. We need to get them involved with the right nation, and that's how God gave me the name "Nu Nation." So in the coming year you'll be hearing a lot more about that.

Believe me, there are no more godly people on this earth than men and women who really know Jesus and live for Him. The very idea that somebody can come in here and steal those godly hearts and souls away is unforgivable. I won't be a party to that. Satan is stealing our young people. He's stealing our fathers; he's killing our mothers and breaking their hearts. But, I'm sorry to say, he's doing it because we've been sleeping.

The enemy is selling false pride that is dangerous and self-destructive. People have no fear of God; they have no God to believe in. So somebody is selling them a bill of goods in the name of a false religion, and they're not sure what to believe anymore.

But let me tell you, I've got the answer! Jesus is the answer, and He's the only answer that really works. He is the only answer that will save your life. I'm saying, Call on Him! He is the way, the truth, and the life, and His name is not Mohammed or Buddha or Hare Krishna. It's Jesus, and He loves you.

WORDS AND MUSIC

I believe that all the drama I've experienced in my life is because God wanted me to have a sensitivity to the music and to people's pain. I believe that what you live is going to dictate what you play and what you write.

And I believe that your motives will dictate what happens. If you're there because it's a gig and just because you're going to get a check for it, then you're not going to touch the hearts of the people. But if you're there because you've been there yourself—been there, done that, gone through some hard times and come through them with a sense of blessing—then I believe you can touch somebody's heart.

It's as if you say with your lyrics, "Want to hear about it? I'm glad you asked."

When we went back on the road in December 1996 after six weeks off, there was a new focus to what we were doing. Now and then a preacher or another brother I respected would come up to me after a show and say, "Man, you've really got a crazy anointing on you now!" In other words, they thought they could feel the Holy Spirit in our performance in a way they'd never felt it before.

I can't say whether the performance changed. Honestly, I don't think it has. But what I have seen is that when I get the microphone now and it's time to say a word and minister to the people, I feel the hand of the Lord like I never did before. It is an anointing.

People want to say I'm some sort of new man, a new entertainer, and that this is all new with me, but I can't see that that's really the case. If it is, I certainly can't see it. It's nothing the physical eye can see. It's something only God can see, and possibly a few others who walk closely with Him. But I'm just walking day by day and doing what I can to thank Him and serve Him with the music.

The first big song we ever had was "Why We Sing," and I think that song puts a lot of this into perspective. It says:

Someone asked the question, why do we sing;
When we lift our hands to Jesus, what do we really mean?
Someone may be wondering, when we sing our song;
At times we may be crying and nothing's even wrong.
I sing because I'm happy. I sing because I'm free,
His eye is on the sparrow. That's the reason why I sing.

And when the song is over, we've all said Amen,
In your heart, just keep on singing, and the song will
never end.

And if somebody asks you, was it just a show?
Lift your hands and be a witness, and tell the
whole world no.
And when we've crossed that river, to study war no more,
We will sing our song to Jesus, the One whom we adore.
I sing because I'm happy. I sing because I'm free,
His eye is on the sparrow. That's the reason why I sing.
Glory, hallelujah, You're the reason why I sing!
Glory, hallelujah, You're the reason why I sing!
Glory, hallelujah, I give the praises to You.
Glory, hallelujah, You're the reason why I sing!

What motivates me is the knowledge that God has redeemed me from the pain and the hurts and the sin of my past and given me a new joy I can't even explain. It's not just for show. It's the truth, and that's what I want to express. I want to write the unwriteable, to compose the unheard melodies, to create the perfect song of praise, to touch the very heart of God.

I really have a whole different viewpoint than most people do when it comes to songwriting. I don't say this trying to be too deep. I say it out of safety and because it's where I feel most comfortable. I don't believe I have ever written a song.

I believe that I am a pen. I believe that God is the Poet, and the people are the paper. The pen cannot tell the Poet what to write. The pen only writes what the Poet has to say, and the pen should never get the credit from the paper. The credit should always go back to the Poet.

Because the pen was just an instrument in the Poet's hand.

One reason I believe this is that there are songs that I feel I had nothing to do with, that God just threw down. They just came out. And I don't believe it's because I've got skills. I believe it's because there was a message He wanted me to get out at that particular time and at that particular point in my life.

Now, I know there are people who will say, "But what about the people who don't believe in God who are song-writers?" And I can only say, That's them, that's their lives. I'm talking about me. I believe that, for me, this is how it works.

I enjoy hearing God say the unspeakable things and then writing them down. I like to be able to hear and experience things that people were not even there to write.

The song I've used for the title of this chapter is one God gave me for the new album. It says, "When I cannot hear a melody and I can't feel the sparrows sing . . ." Instead of saying "feel a melody" and "hear the sparrows sing," it's the other way around. That's different. Normally we only hear a sparrow's song; we don't think we feel it, but that's the way it came to me.

The line after that says, "There's a secret place that's full of grace; there's a blessing in the storm." Then the sec-ond verse says, "When the sickness won't leave my body, and the pain won't leave my soul, I get on my knees and say, 'Jesus, please!' because there's a blessing in the storm."

Now, I'm talking about the fact that there's joy in going through stuff. Remember the words of James? "My brothers, count it all joy when you fall into various trials, knowing that the testing of your faith produces patience. But let patience have its perfect work, that you may be perfect and complete, lacking nothing" (James 1:2–4). You know, that's an incredible thought!

But that kind of thinking doesn't make a bit of sense in this world. Only a Christian could make any sense out of that kind of talk. And maybe that's why so many people think we're all crazy!

But it's true, so very true. It's a message God wants us to understand, and I think that's why He gave me this song.

That's what I enjoy: the music and the words coming together.

I am grateful for the music. I honestly think that for me it has been an incredible opportunity to express who I am, a young man who has something to say. I'm not saying that I'm where I need to be or that I've already arrived, but that I'm working hard to get there.

I don't want to just play a part, to give lip service but live an empty life. I don't want to wake up one day and realize that everybody else is getting to know Jesus but I didn't make it.

You know, when it's all said and done, there are going to be some people who won others to Christ but won't be spending eternity with Him themselves because they never claimed that gospel truth for themselves. Isn't that a horrible thought? Some people who know all the right words and have lived in the church all their lives are going to be on the outside looking in because they never really claimed the promise of eternal life for themselves. They may have walked the aisle and they may have sung the songs, but that isn't enough. Only humble repentance before the cross can do it.

There are times when life can be too much and you want to quit. I know that. There are times when it's easy to cave in and go along with stuff that God hates. I know that too. But if you can claim what Jesus is offering and let Him turn you around in a new direction, then you have real peace with God. And even in the storms of life, God's blessing will see you through.

My desire is to please You,
To be more and more like You, Jesus.
Each and every day,
I lift my hands and say,
I want to be more like You.

I give You my life;
Take me in Your arms and hold me, Jesus;
I give You my heart;
I know that You can mend these broken pieces.

I'm totally . . .
I'm totally . . .
Totally committed to You.

I give You my life,
My heart,
My soul.
Take control!

I love You,
I love You.

10

Totally Committed

I wonder if I'll ever get to the point where I can go into the studio and work on a song and not worry whether people will like it. Wow! That's who I want to be. Not to worry, just to know that I'm living everything I'm putting down in the music. And to know that, even if nobody else applauds, at least God has applauded. I could rest in that. To be that kind of artist and a man of God! That would be my dream come true.

People's expectations, from a musical standpoint, are so high now that I have a lot to live up to. It's frustrating to know that so many people are looking at me and saying, "What's he going to do next?"

I feel like saying, "Stop looking at me!"

Can you picture this? It's like a scene from an old movie. There I am on top of the Empire State Building with searchlights shining up there, lighting up the sky, and helicopters buzzing around me and I'm yelling, "Stop looking at me!" That's what I feel like saying. "Stop looking at me!"

Musicians and other creative people are wired a little differently from most folks. We're sensitive to what people think about our work, and we're especially sensitive to criticism. This is a profession where we put our heart and soul on the line every day for anybody and everybody to judge. The audiences can either like what we do or they can hate it. As long as enough of them enjoy it enough of the time, we can keep doing it; but that's always subject to change. But Jesus never changes, so He's the one I'm striving to please.

If it ever changes, then it will be time to go back and take another look at what we're doing. At least, that would be the smart thing from a business perspective; but there's also an emotional side to this business, and that's where I am most of the time. I like to think that the anointing on our music means more to us than our desire for applause and approval. But we're all human, and we are driven to perform music that people respond to.

This is an area I have to pray through and think about in my quiet times with God, not allowing other people's opinions to sway what I feel. Sometimes I ask for people's opinions on how I did before I ask God how I did. It's my human nature. But I have to remember that the One I really want to please is the One I'm here to serve, and if He can use my life and my music to glorify His Son, Jesus Christ, then I'm satisfied.

Keeping those two sides in balance is a constant struggle. And that's why I can't allow myself to get caught up in all the trappings of success. There's still so much work to be done on Kirk, I ain't got time for that stuff!

I'm not where I want to be. But I don't say I've got more growing to do; it's more like I have more *dying* to do.

Dying to self and working each day to maintain a humble heart. Here I am in a place in my life where people are telling me how good we are, how important our music is, and what great ministers of the gospel we are, and I'm thinking, *That's probably the last thing any of us needs to hear.*

Encouragement is good, and it helps us know what the audience thinks of us; but one night after the show in New York City, I felt the Lord telling me to go on a fast. Not a food fast, a media fast. He wants me to stop looking at my reviews and stop seeing all the praise we get when we're performing so that we can keep things in proper balance and perspective.

He wants me to stop it all for a while and not look at all the wonderful things people are saying. He wants me to concentrate on Him and my walk because He's got some moves I need to concentrate on. I've got to be able to hear His still, small voice, and that's not easy to do in the middle of a circus.

The reality of the situation is that I'm a Christian in a non-Christian environment. The majority of the stuff I'm doing is happening in the secular marketplace. For example, I got a call from MTV asking me to host the Top Ten Countdown, and I had to say no. That's not right for me. That's not my message or my ministry. I can't introduce a video that says, "I want to sex you up!" God is not going to honor that, and that's the most important thing I have to think about. What matters to me is, What does God want Kirk Franklin to be?

As a musician, I want to know that I'm pleasing most of the crowd most of the time. That's important for a lot of good reasons. By nature I'm a pleaser, so I feel bad if I think people aren't satisfied with my work. Maybe I'll grow out of that or maybe I won't, but right now it's something I struggle with.

My biggest hope for the future is to have some peace of mind and, one day, some rest. How I'd love to be able to sit down and read through my Bible without my mind racing ahead thinking of fifty other things! How I'd love to stretch out somewhere with a good book, with no interruptions, so I wouldn't have to go back and reread the same paragraph over and over again.

It's frustrating to be so preoccupied that I can never focus on the things that matter, especially knowing that half the stuff I'm worrying about isn't even important!

A SENSE OF PURPOSE

Sometimes we will go into a hall for a concert and have eleven or twelve thousand people there (which is an awesome crowd for a gospel concert), and I feel a real sense of responsibility knowing that this may be the only chance anybody will ever have to touch some of those people with the gospel. We don't want to be pushy, but we don't want to miss the opportunity either. Somebody's eternal life may be at stake.

Many times when we've been doing a concert and praising the Lord and worshiping in a large crowd, I've wished that the gift of healing could take place. I've prayed over people and laid hands on some of them and asked for them to be healed of some condition or illness or financial situation, but to the best of my knowledge it hasn't happened. At least, not at that moment. But I rest in the knowledge that the gift of music is being used to awaken people to their needs.

If we can just do that night after night and bring even a hundred people to the point where they realize that Jesus really is the answer, then maybe that's the best we can do. And as much as I would like to see miracles happen in those crowds, I know my real calling is to be faithful to what God has given me to do. I want to be the best musician and the best witness of His grace that I can be. Then I just have to leave the rest to Him.

At the end of each concert I try to make a time for people either to recommit their lives to Christ or, as happens now in a growing number of cases, to give their hearts to Him for the first time. Obviously, we don't have the staff or the counseling expertise to take it much further than that, but we can start the process.

I tell those who come forward to claim salvation in faith and then to find a good Bible-believing church where they can be discipled and ministered to. Generally, that's as far as we can go. We're seed planters, not harvesters. We have to trust the Spirit to lead them to a place where they can grow in the faith.

It may be that out of a hundred people who come down to the front at the end of a concert, no more than fifty or sixty will actually take the next step and begin a sincere walk with the Lord. But I take comfort in the knowledge that it's fifty or sixty more than it would have been if we hadn't been there that night.

I understand that some people just get caught up in the emotion and come forward because others are doing it, and nothing will really change in their lives. I know that happens. I'm sure it happens in Billy Graham crusades and at altar calls every Sunday. But who knows how the seed we've planted may start growing a month, a year, or even ten years down the road? We don't create the harvest. We just trust God for the increase.

God spoke through the prophet Isaiah when he said, "My thoughts are not your thoughts, nor are your ways My ways" (Isaiah 55:8). We don't need to question what He's doing; He knows. We just have to be faithful to the calling we've been given.

Later, Paul said, "Eye has not seen, nor ear heard, nor have entered into the heart of man the things which God has prepared for those who love Him" (1 Corinthians 2:9). I love that verse, and I really warm to its message. God has got something so incredible laid up for His children, we can't even begin to imagine how awesome it's going to be!

We touch those we can, and knowing that there are a lot of church people in the crowd most nights, we hope some of those people may be able to reach out to the ones who come forward.

I remember one night when three women came up to the front separately and said they'd just found out they had

AIDS, and they asked for prayer. Of course, I said I would pray for them, but that's a serious responsibility.

The only way I can do it is to pray immediately and to say, "Dear God, please bless this woman and heal her of the disease according to Your will and the faith You've given to her." If I don't do it right then, I may forget to pray later and break a promise. So I've learned that I need to pray right then, whenever possible.

One of the most amazing concerts we ever did was in Detroit, Michigan, in 1995. We were getting close to the end of the show, and everything was going just great. I had asked those who wanted to get right with Jesus to come forward, but so many people started coming down the aisles to give their lives to Him that the crowd up front overfilled the capacity.

Most of the auditoriums we perform in are union halls, so we have to be finished and out of there right on time or we can get charged a lot of money, and the promoters don't like that at all. This particular night there were so many people up front giving their hearts to Christ, I realized we had a problem and we were going to get stuck with a big bill.

But the Holy Spirit was moving and people were being blessed, so I wasn't going to break it up over money. Instead I was led to do something I've never done before or since, and I know it was the Holy Spirit speaking to me. He told me to ask for money.

I never do that. I find it hard to do that for myself, let alone in a concert crowd that size. So when the Lord spoke to my heart, I prayed, "Lord, You know what You're doing, and You know what You want to do tonight. So bless my words."

I took the microphone and said, "Ladies and gentlemen, we've gone overtime, and it's going to cost us some money. Now, I'm not going to beg, but if you've been blessed tonight and if you don't mind helping me pay this overtime bill, would you help us out?"

Before I even got the words out of my mouth, money started falling from the balcony. People were throwing ten- and twenty-dollar bills down on the stage. Everywhere I looked there was money raining down on us, and people were passing it up to the stage. I've never seen anything like it in my entire life. I had never asked for money on the road, and now folks were running up to the stage putting money up there for us. I didn't know what to do.

So I looked back at Jessie Hurst and said, "Jessie, send somebody up here to get the money." I didn't even want to touch it.

As I said earlier, I've never felt the Lord speak to me about healing or anything of that kind, but every now and then the gift of prophecy will come. I believe the Bible is trustworthy, and I believe in the gifts of the Spirit. I mean, if it's in the Bible, I believe it. So when the Lord spoke to me, I listened.

That night He also told me there was a woman there who was flat broke and had absolutely nothing left. He told me this woman and her kids were just about to be evicted from their apartment and had no place to go. He said to help her.

With that on my mind, the Lord then led me to speak to the people, and I said, "I believe that God is telling us to be a blessing to someone tonight." So I told them about the woman I felt the Lord had laid on my heart, and I said, "We're going to take some of the money you've given tonight and bless that woman, whoever she is."

Well, I had no way of knowing any of that by human wisdom. For all I knew, there could have been a hundred women in the audience that night who matched the description. And all of them might come up at once and claim their blessing.

But God had said that there was a woman, and only one woman came up and told me she was the one I had just described. In my spirit, I knew she was the one. Afterward, she told me her story, and I stood there in tears while she told me what was happening to her; it was exactly as I had described it on stage.

She said it wasn't even her idea to come to see us that night. She had come on a church bus with a bunch of other people who insisted that she come along and receive a blessing from God. She said she didn't want to come because she didn't have anything to wear, so her friend had loaned her the dress she was wearing.

She didn't have any idea what was going to happen to her, but when I spoke those words she knew that God had singled her out, that He had called her out of a crowd of thousands of people to receive a blessing.

When we counted out the money the audience had showered on us, it turned out to be exactly enough to pay the union overtime and to give that woman the precise amount she said she needed to pay the rent and take care of her immediate debts. Brother, when something like that happens, you better believe God is right in the middle of it!

WHEN THE SPIRIT MOVES

When God moves, you can feel it all over the house, and I think we all felt His hand that night. I usually warn the audience at the start of the show that this is going to be a new experience for some of them. I won't always have to do that; sooner or later people are going to know what to expect when they come to our concerts.

But honestly, there's always going to be something in me, whenever we do a show or a live concert, that wants to tell people to get ready. I don't like getting too comfortable. I hate routine, and I don't want my music to become so familiar that people will know what to expect and there are no new surprises.

I enjoy getting up in front of the people, taking them on this musical experience, and at the end of the road, right before they get off the roller coaster, asking them if they know the Lord. That's very special, and the journey getting there is also fun. The chance to create a whole musical experience is an incredible opportunity and privilege, and I don't take it lightly.

Getting from town to town and dealing with all the arrangements and hassles that go with it, now *that* can be strenuous! I don't like that part. Waking up in the morning and catching another plane. That's tough. But as far as ministering in song is concerned, I count it as a privilege.

The interaction with the Family, horsing around, telling stories, cracking jokes, and all the silly stuff backstage is always a lot of fun. I'm not a heavy-handed leader. I don't like getting down on people or yelling. Now and then we may have a disagreement or two or somebody may let the group down by showing up late or maybe not showing up at all, and then I have to say something. But that's the part of my job I like the least.

I don't have the kind of temperament to keep riding people who don't pull their share, so if it happens very often I may have to let them go. I wish it didn't have to be that way. For the most part, everybody in our camp knows how things are, and they bend over backward to make it work.

A few Contemporary Christian music stations are playing our music now, but I don't foresee any big changes until there's a better dialogue between blacks and whites in this country. There is still a racial problem. I know the church is trying to deal with it. Promise Keepers has been trying to deal with it, and there are some signs of a movement. But it's not finished yet, and we're still a long way from solving the problems. In the meantime, I'm not sure my music is going to cross over to a general audience.

Somebody told me that during our preview concert in New York there was a whole section of white people in the audience, and they were getting into it as much as anybody in the house. That doesn't happen a lot, but I think it's great when it does. God doesn't pay attention to color. The

Bible says He's no respecter of persons. So if He can use my music to bring people together, then I'm all for it!

If it happens, wonderful. But people are going to have to make decisions. I often feel that gospel music and what I'm doing are never going to be that popular. The reason is because if people really listen to this music, then they're going to have to start making some decisions about Jesus, and I don't know how many of them are ready for that.

But I can see that God is moving. Take, for example, the story of our keyboard player, Bobby Sparks, one of the most outstanding musicians I have ever known. When we're rolling with Bobby on the keys, Jerome Allen on bass, and Erik Morgan on the drums, anything can happen. Bobby has been with me since day one, but he just gave his life to the Lord a few days before we started our New York tour in August 1997.

When people remember you back when, when they know all the dirt on you and they've seen you do wrong, and when they finally see Jesus in you and receive your message, to me that's the greatest testimony imaginable. For people to know you and to know all your junk and to see that Jesus is moving in you, that's really important.

Imagine my feelings when I saw Bobby come down from the keyboard one night and stand there in front of the stage with all the others who had come forward that night. What an awesome sensation ran through my mind! Here was a man I truly loved, who had been with me from the start. It took all that time for him to realize that Jesus is the only way, the only truth, and the only life that really matters and to come down from the stage and give His heart to Jesus. Not in Dallas, not in New York, but in Birmingham, Alabama, in the middle of our tour.

I think Bobby's decision really started at the hotel earlier that day. He was always the guy who just had no limits. We were sitting around talking about something we were going to do that night at the concert. He was trying to explain something to me, and I just wasn't getting it.

Finally, he said, "Oh, man, just forget it."

It was as if he was saying there was something wrong with him because he couldn't explain what he meant.

I said, "There's nothing wrong with you, Bobby. There are some things in your life that you need to get straight.

I don't usually say stuff like that—that's the kind of thing your mother might say. But I had a special place in my heart for him.

At one point I said, "Bobby, you have an awesome gift, and you've got all this talent. But it's not submitted to the Lord." Bobby did a double take; those words had an effect on him, and he was thinking about that.

Then I said, "Gifts and calling come with repentance, Bobby. Peter said, 'Repent, and let every one of you be baptized in the name of Jesus Christ for the remission of sins; and you shall receive the gift of the Holy Spirit' [Acts 2:38]. So if you want the gift, you have to give up anything that's holding you back from God." I did not say that to Bobby because I had a closer relationship to him; I've been where Bobby was and I knew what he needed.

I guess Bobby took those words to heart, and that night I saw the fruit of our conversation. But I was as surprised as anyone—expect maybe Bobby—to see him go down front and give his life to Christ. That moment stands out as one of the highlights of my ministry, and now Bobby's not just my black brother and a fellow musician but also a brother in Christ.

TAKING CARE OF BUSINESS

In a group like ours, teamwork is very important, and that's especially true when the object is to serve God and point people to Jesus. Every member of the Family is important to me, and every voice brings something to our sound that is essential.

Losing one voice changes our balance, and when one of the band members is off or not with us, it has an effect on our performance. So I work very hard to keep the strength and unity of the team, and I felt that Bobby's decision made Kirk Franklin & the Family a stronger team.

I've had people try to run my thing, to sort of push things one direction or another, but they didn't last long. It wasn't a yell-fight thing—we don't do much of that—but we all knew they had to go. Our team leaders all work that way.

Jessie Hurst is a tough manager, but he's not mean. The guys who run the boards and make the stage show happen can be demanding and loud when they have to, but they're with us all the way. Every one of those people contributes something important to the impact of our performance. I'm convinced they're all handpicked by God to be doing what they're doing and to be doing it with us.

The biggest challenge I have is trying to get away from what other people are saying about me, because sometimes what other people want me to be may not be what God wants me to be. I honestly hate looking in the mirror. It doesn't matter how much I pray or how much time I spend before God, it's always a challenge to maintain focus and to be objective about this ministry.

It seems like I'm always on the run, constantly going, never taking a vacation. Tammy and I had to wait five months into our marriage to have a honeymoon. When our first album took off, we were running as hard as we could to keep up with it, and since then there has been very little time for ourselves. When you're on the roller coaster you can't just step off anytime you feel like it, but people tell me that I've got to change that. Cells have to rebuild, muscles have to rest, and my spirit needs a retreat now and then to renew and refresh.

Even the things I like to do I have to keep in check. I like to go to the mall, to go shopping, but that's not always being a good steward. So a lot of time I have to check that. Learning what to do and what not to do with God's money is very important to me. Until the day I die, I'll be convinced that this is God's money. Because of that, just because I see something I like or even that I need, that doesn't necessarily mean I should have it. So

I have to weigh that, to be sure it's right and that God approves, then do the right thing with the resources He has given to me.

What's happening now is that I'm learning how to enjoy my family. I'm beginning to find my peace with my wife and children and to just enjoy this beautiful relationship God has given me as a husband and father. When we're not on the road, I try to take Mondays off to spend with my family. That's family day.

Recently I read an article about accountability among Christian leaders, particularly black leaders in the church. The writer was Bishop Larry Trotter of Chicago. It was a powerful word from a brother who's a little older than I am but who has an awesome heart for God, and he said what every Christian leader needs to hear.

The primary focus of the article was about sex and the ministry, and he got very transparent and very honest with the readers. He took off his bishop shirt and just got real. I said I needed to meet this man, so we got together. It has been a great experience for me to meet and fellowship with someone like Bishop Trotter, who has seen the truth and is willing to go on the record for what has become such an important issue today.

Accountability is important. I'm glad to say that Fred Hammond, who is one of the most important gospel singers of the last fifty years, has become a close personal friend. We have a mentoring, fostering relationship with one another; we're accountable to each other. Fred really knows what it means to live out in your private life what you say you believe in public. Fred is what he seems to be all the time, and I love that about him.

As I said in the first chapters of this book, I wasn't the most popular guy around when I was growing up. I wasn't a standout in a crowd, I wasn't picked for the teams, I wasn't admired by the girls. The young men everybody liked were the hard guys, the macho guys, and I wasn't like that. I wasn't somebody everybody wanted to hang out with.

But there were a number of guys I hung around with when I was growing up, and two of them started calling me a couple of years ago when our records were getting popular. They would leave messages and want me to call back.

Now, I knew these kids when I was very young. But when we got into junior high and high school, we drifted apart and hardly ever saw each other anymore. They were both good-looking guys, extremely popular with the girls, and of course I wasn't. So there was no reason for them to keep track of me, and eventually they lost interest.

These guys knew me. We went to church together, went to the movies together, but when they got popular and busy they stopped calling. So now that I'm better known and my music has been successful, they start calling me all the time. But before long word got back to me that these guys were saying things about me behind my back.

I'm very busy and on the road a lot, so I don't have time to talk to most people, especially to those who never had time for me back then. But one of these guys left a nasty message on my answering machine, and he had an attitude because I hadn't had a chance to call him back.

So I called him and said, "What's your problem?"

He said, "You're acting like you're some kind of big shot now. You never call anybody."

I'm thinking, *Am I hearing what I think I'm hearing? What is this guy thinking?* We knew each other years ago, but we hadn't spoken since the tenth grade. Now he was upset because I wouldn't return his calls? Excuse me, but where was he when I needed a friend? Where was he when I was sitting home every night? So I finally called back and said, "Forgive me if I don't return your calls. It's been far too long, and there's far too much water under that old bridge."

Those kinds of things still happen, but they're not the real challenge. The real challenge is to be able to trust God enough to know that He's going to supply for the ministry. I've got full-time people with me, and sometimes we have to keep things running to be able to keep everybody working. That's a challenge because I don't want to see them stuck. When we get over that hurdle, I hope I can slow down and take some time off.

FOR THE FUTURE

We have a new album coming out in 1998, and we're all excited about that. If God gives it His blessing, that will be great. From a musical standpoint, we want to grow and develop what we've got. That means adding other kinds of music, other techniques and other media and seeing where else we can go with it.

Up to this point we've done some innovative things, but we've been pretty much at home in the world of gospel music. There are bits of jazz and rock in our music with traditional instruments—keyboard, drums, bass, horns, and that sort of thing. But now I'd like to reach out a little bit with strings, a symphony orchestra, and other types of sound. I believe that a lot of exciting things can happen if we're willing to push out of our comfort zone.

So the album we will release in 1998 will be the most sensitive, intimate, personal record that God has ever allowed me to be a part of, and we've been working on it for more than half a year now. As this book goes to press, the album isn't quite finished, but it's on the way. Pulling it together has taken every bit of knowledge I have because there are so many different pieces to it.

This album represents every style of music in our culture—jazz, gospel, blues, hip-hop, rock, ballads, blues, classical, you name it. They say music is universal, but the message is specific. If this music is universal, it's all ours; it's the message within it that makes the difference. Gospel music fans may be surprised at first. I'm afraid there may be some who won't like it because it's different. But I hope they'll give us a chance to show them that our hearts haven't changed. We're still the same people; we just feel that God has given us a chance to grow and expand our reach. It's different, but it's all dedicated to Him.

There's not just one gospel sound. The gospel is the

message, and as long as the music is dedicated to Jesus, He makes it pure. Whatever music we put with the message, whether it's drums or guitars or a full symphony orchestra, He purifies it. That's what He does. He gives it a ministry.

So that's something I'm pretty excited about, and nervous about too. Incorporating all those styles can be risky; but this is the first time in my life that I've had a chance to be totally involved in a project from every aspect. I'm in this record from the ground up.

Over the last few years, I've written a lot of songs for other albums—for people like Myrna Summer, Lawrence Matthews, Daryl Coley, James Moore, and a half-dozen gospel choirs. I've already said that one of my songs was picked up for the movie *The Preacher's Wife*, and that helped us in the beginning.

I'd like to do more of that, but I'd also like to do some interludes, film scores, and instrumental numbers that are a little bit different from anything we've tried up to now. I want to stretch Kirk Franklin, stretch our sound, and maybe even stretch the audience too. Those are some of the things I'm working on now.

In the middle of all this, our *God's Property* album was nominated in four categories for Grammy Awards, and we're still getting invitations to perform on network TV shows, in large concerts, and for many other events around the country. We're not touring in 1998 because there's so much going on, but we expect to be back on the road in 1999.

Church Boy

THE KIRK FRANKLIN SHOW

One of the most exciting times for me is when I had the opportunity to do a pilot for a sitcom. It was another situation that was a little bit touchy because some people have said they don't think a twenty-eight-year-old minister (as I am) should be doing a Hollywood sitcom. But, I felt the pluses far outweighed the minuses, and if it was God's will, I wasn't going to stand in the way.

There are some people in the church who seem to think that Christians shouldn't laugh and have fun, so we may get some ridicule, some bad press, or some controversy out of it. The character I played felt good in my spirit, and I thought it would be good, not only for the body of Christ, but for the general public. It showed somebody who was more than just a stereotyped Bible-toting, Scripture-quoting, black-suit-wearing saint. He had a little edge on him, and it was a really good part.

My character in the pilot was a Hollywood record producer who's down on his luck a little bit. He has a list of records that haven't done very well; he also has some back-tax problems and some money problems, and he's not doing quite as well as he would like.

Actually, nobody really knows how badly he's struggling except for himself and his manager, but when things slow down he decides to move back home to Chicago and stay with his sister for a while. At one point he goes over to the old church where he used to be a member to see what's happening, and he finds that it's struggling too. Things aren't really rolling in the church; membership is down, and there's not much spirit, so he agrees to help out with the choir.

You see, he grew up in the church, but when he got into the music scene and became a big R&B producer, he lost touch with it. So that's the dynamic. He's there, loving the kids, helping with the youth choir, and helping out the pastor; but he has regular problems like we all do. This character also becomes transparent an does not come across as perfect. He shows that we all stumble and fall, but as a young Christian brother, he gets back up..

It shows that we all have imperfections, and if we're going to touch Generation X, we've got to admit we're not perfect.

There aren't too many spiritual leaders these days who are willing to let down their guard and show that they make mistakes just like everybody else. They don't want people to know that they kick and yell if their team loses the Super Bowl or that they get angry at their kids and say things they shouldn't say. I truly believe that's why a lot of people never try Christianity—either because they assume they've got to be perfect to be a Christian or because they've seen Christians make mistakes then fail to admit their weaknesses.

So, besides all the fun and good humor in the show, there's a message for those who have ears to hear. We conducted a talent search to find the young people for the choir. The choir is multi-racial, and I think that's a wonderful idea. The church is in a mixed neighborhood, and the pastor is white, so a lot of the chemistry and the humor grow out of this cross-cultural mix.

I think that's great, because it's bridging some gaps and helping to put band-aids on some old wounds. It's a chance to do something that's both fun and creative that will also have a wholesome message. I must say, there are times when it's a little intimidating working with all those Hollywood producers and executives who have so many hit shows under their belts, but I've enjoyed every minute of it.

I had an agreement to do a sitcom with UPN back in 1996, but I eventually had to bail out of the contract. In one episode, they wanted me to say that it was okay if one of the cast members was gay. I was supposed to say, "That's perfectly normal," and I couldn't agree to that. I am not homophobic, and I don't hate gay people, but I believe it is a choice, a wrong choice, and that Jesus has the power to repair the hurts in our hearts that lead to that kind of behavior.

I tried to convince the producer of the series to rewrite the part so that my character could show concern for this gay person by doing something positive, like saving him from an angry mob. But they wouldn't go for it, so I told them the deal was off. That was the end of that one, but it was just a matter of weeks before we got the call from Universal to take a look at this new program. My agents put together a contract, and now we're doing a much better show with a much better concept, and I don't have to say anything I don't really believe.

Kirk Franklin

FANNING THE FLAMES

The Bible says, "My people are destroyed for lack of knowledge" (Hosea 4:6). I think that's especially true in the black community today. Other stuff has taken our eyes off the prize, and we've let sin and lust and violence soak into everything we do. Ignorance is killing us, but it doesn't have to be that way.

First of all, I'm fully committed to keeping my own life in balance, which means putting God first, my family second, and my work third. I know that strategy works because I've seen it happen. As long as I keep those things at the top of my list and in that order, I know God will be honored and everything else will come out the way He wants it to.

I just celebrated a couple of very important anniversaries in my life. It's been over a year now since I fell off the stage in Memphis, and that's an important landmark. It's a feeling of relief to know the accident is mostly behind me now. During the recuperation, my doctors said I needed to be careful for the first year because there was still a chance I could have a seizure or something. But it didn't happen and, praise God, the only time I've been back to the hospital since the fall was for the birth of our daughter, Kennedy.

Tammy and I celebrated our second wedding anniversary on January 20, 1998, and my love for my wife is stronger today than ever before. My desire to be a better father and husband has grown stronger. I've grown so attached to Tammy and all three of our kids. My family—

that's my life! Other than Jesus, that's what I wake up for each day, and that's what I'm working for. I can't find words to explain what my family means to me.

Tammy is my best friend. She's somebody I can laugh with and play with. I mean, we take care of business together; we solve problems together; we raise the kids together; and sometimes we have water fights and run around the house chasing each other like little kids, just acting silly. It means so much to have that kind of committed, loving, and permanent relationship bound by a strong bond of marriage and our faith in God.

The biggest event for me in the near future will be the Nu Nation Convention in the year 2000. If God provides the opportunity and the right leadership along the way, it will be a major event and generate a lot of interest from all over the world. I hope to get young people from every continent and hundreds of nations to come together for a week for fellowship, for fun, and for learning, teaching, and workshops that will hold their interest.

Very soon we're going to announce the formation of Nu Nation chapters in every major city, with organized programs and an annual board meeting in the winter. We want to get youth pastors from around the country to take part and help us provide creative ideas for reaching young people. I believe that revival can come to this nation if God's people will focus on the basics. I truly believe it will come, but not from the old leadership. It will come from young people themselves, and I believe it will come from Generation X.

I'm doing all the things I do because I truly believe. I sing what I sing because I know there's hope. I go where I go because all over this planet there are people who need to know that God is love and that Jesus is His Son. If I can break people's hearts and touch them with music and laughter and love so that they'll know that, "Yeah, there *is* a better way," then I've accomplished what I'm here for.

God only knows where I'll be tomorrow. Only He knows what Kirk Franklin will do in the next ten years. But I'm on fire now and fanning the flames as fast as I can because, as I said in my one moment of glory at Eastern Hills Elementary School all those years ago, "I have a dream." Dr. King's dream was that all God's children could be free and equal. My dream is that all free people will come to know Jesus.

Music is not the only way to do that, but it's one way. And it's the way He has given me. So I'm ready, wherever He takes me from here! Can I get a witness?!